THE
ENGLAND
CRICKET
MISCELLANY

This edition published in 2006

Copyright © Carlton Books Limited 2006

Carlton Books Limited
20 Mortimer Street
London W1T 3JW

A CIP catalogue record for this book is available from the British Library

ISBN 10:1-84442-161-9
ISBN 13:978-1-84442-161-9

Editor: Martin Corteel
Project Art Editor: Darren Jordan
Production: Lisa French

Printed in Great Britain

THE

ENGLAND CRICKET

MISCELLANY

JOHN WHITE

WITH A FOREWORD BY GEOFFREY BOYCOTT, OBE

CARLTON
BOOKS

▓

◦ LIST OF ABBREVIATIONS ◦

CBE	Commander (of the Order) of the British Empire
CCC	County Cricket Club
CCI	Cricket Club of India
ECB	England & Wales Cricket Board
ECC	European Cricket Council
FC	Football Club
ICC	International Cricket Conference
MCC	Marylebone Cricket Club
MCG	Marylebone Cricket Ground
OBE	Order of the British Empire
ODI	One-Day International
TCCB	Test and County Cricket Board

▥

⟳ FOREWORD BY GEOFFREY BOYCOTT ⟳

Many of the proudest moments of my life have been on cricket pitches around the world. There is something very special, on the first day of a Test match, walking out to the middle wearing an England sweater and cap. What honour can be greater than to represent your country at the pinnacle of your chosen sport? In 1977 for me to score my one hundredth first class century in a Test match against Australia at Headingley was very special. It doesn't get any better than that.

I was determined from a very young age to be the best I could. I remember going to watch Tom Graveney bat and to learn from him. How many of today's players did exactly the same, finding a hero and watching him play almost oblivious to the rest of the game. The wonderful sport of cricket has given me the opportunity to do and see things that otherwise would have been impossible.

When John White approached me to write this foreword, I was delighted. Cricket has become popular again, much as in the early 1980s, with Andrew Flintoff taking the Ian Botham role as Ashes hero. John's book is not just about the Ashes, or England winning that series. It is about English cricket in small segments, such as the series record between England and Pakistan, the scorecards from famous matches, lists of England players who captained the team only once; those players who were out hit wicket, and much more. Turning the pages reminded me of players and incidents that I had forgotten and some I never knew.

John tells me he only got interested in cricket in a big way during the Ashes series last summer. Good for him! In many ways he shows the same talents necessary for opening an innings: patience, a good eye for a chance; the good sense to ignore the rubbish; and to follow through when the chance permits.

I wish him every success with his book. It is a superb record of the England team and I warmly recommend it to every England cricket fan.

Geoffrey Boycott, OBE
June 2006

☰
❦ ACKNOWLEDGEMENTS ❧

This book is dedicated to several very special people without whose help I may have been stumped along the way, run out of ideas or simply caught out with several of the facts behind some entries.

To my mate John Dempsey who introduced me to cricket; to Geoffrey Boycott for his wonderful foreword; to Peter Griffiths at www.cricketarchive.com for all of his help and guidance compiling the book; to Rajesh Kumar for his assistance with many of the entries contained within the book; to Rebecca Saleem, Steve Dobell, Chris Marshall and David Ballheimer for their editorial work; to my publisher, Martin Corteel, for having the faith in me to see this project through and for taking the time to help me with various entries for the book and last but certainly not least, to another good friend of mine, Bill Clarkson, for showering all his knowledge and wisdom of cricket on me.

I would also like to thank Colin Creed and the team at www.howstat.com for kindly permitting me to reproduce in my book many of the tables the Howstat team have compiled; Gaurang and the team at India Cricket Fever (www.sportsnetwork.net) for kindly permitting me to reproduce in my book some of the material they have compiled; the Webmaster at www.wikipedia.org for hosting such an informative website covering cricket; Matthew Paton at Christie's Auctions, London; Philip Bailey and Peter Griffiths at www.cricketarchive.com for kindly permitting me to reproduce many of the tables in my book they have compiled, David Roberts at Guinness Publishing Limited; and to Paul at the Barmy Army website - http://www.barmyarmy.com/cricket/contact.asp for permission to reproduce some of the material found on the website. I would also like to express my thanks to one of the unsung heroes at Carlton Publishing and that person is Darren Jordan, the creative genius behind this Miscellany and the others I have written.

Finally, one last note of thanks must go to my mother-in-law and my father-in-law, Ruth and Bobby McWilliams, for all their support and encouragement.

Thanks one and all.

John

III

∽ INTRODUCTION ∽

This book is the natural follow-up to my *England Football Miscellany*. I knew from the moment that Michael, Freddie and the boys beat the Aussies last summer to reclaim the Ashes that I just had to write a cricket book. The euphoria surrounding England's momentous victory is still prevalent today whenever an English batsman takes guard with the famous three lions emblazoned on his shirt. It is the anticipation of what will follow that is so captivating to those in attendance and the millions watching on television.

But what exactly is *The England Cricket Miscellany*? Well, this volume is neither an encyclopaedia, nor a reference book, nor a quiz book, nor a statistics book about English cricket. It is, however, a mixture of all of these, with a sprinkling of quirky entries thrown in that will hopefully please you.

There have been some titanic clashes with old foes such as Australia, India and the West Indies and many outstanding individual performances from England batsmen and bowlers down the years that I have attempted to capture within the pages of my book. Who will ever forget Ian Botham smashing the Australians for 149 not out in the second innings of the third Ashes Test at Headingley in July 1981 before going on to help his team bowl out the Aussies and win a match that the bookmakers at one point had England priced at 500/1 to win? Beefy's performances that summer are recounted in my book along with many other defining moments that have helped shape the history of English cricket both on and off the field.

I would like to think that my book will bowl you over, or perhaps catch you out for a duck, but even if it provides you with a single interesting entry then I have in some way improved your knowledge of the England cricket team.

John White
June 2006

II

⚭ FANTASY ENGLAND XI (1) ⚭

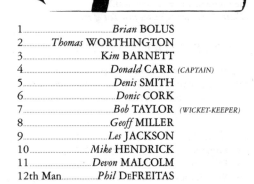

DERBYSHIRE

1	*Brian* BOLUS	
2	*Thomas* WORTHINGTON	
3	*Kim* BARNETT	
4	*Donald* CARR	*(CAPTAIN)*
5	*Denis* SMITH	
6	*Donic* CORK	
7	*Bob* TAYLOR	*(WICKET-KEEPER)*
8	*Geoff* MILLER	
9	*Les* JACKSON	
10	*Mike* HENDRICK	
11	*Devon* MALCOLM	
12th Man	*Phil* DeFREITAS	

Did You Know That?

Derbyshire CCC joined the County Championship in 1895 with three others, Essex, Hampshire and Warwickshire. In 1920, Derbyshire lost every single match they played, but success came in 1936, when they won their first, and to date only, County Championship.

⚭ DR VAUGHAN ⚭

On 8 February 2006 Michael Vaughan was awarded an honorary doctorate by his local university, Sheffield Hallam, in a special event at Sheffield City Hall. His honorary doctorate was actually announced live on Radio 4's *Test Match Special* on the day he scored 166 runs in the third Test match at Old Trafford, which ended in a draw. Michael was unable to receive his degree during the university's graduation ceremonies, because he was in Pakistan with the England team.

⚭ DEMON ENDS W.G. GRACE'S CAREER ⚭

In May 1878 "The Demon Bowler", F.R. Spofforth of Australia, one of the greatest Test cricketers of the nineteenth century, took 6 wickets for 4 runs and then a further 4 wickets for 16 runs against the MCC at Lord's. Spofforth is regarded as being the player who brought down the curtain on the career of the legendary W.G. Grace.

III

⟿ ASHES FEVER (1) ⟿

"I think I was saying 3–0 or 4–0 about 12 months ago, thinking there might be a bit of rain around. But with the weather as it is at the moment I have to say 5–0."
Glenn McGrath *before the first Test of the 2005 Ashes*

⟿ TOP NATIONS BY WIN PERCENTAGES ⟿

England lie second in the table of Test-playing nations by win percentage with 54.86%. Here is the table up to and including games played on 22 September 2005:

Pos.	Team	Matches	Won	Lost	Drawn	Tied	% Won*
1.	Australia	670	304	178	186	2	63.07
2.	**England**	**839**	**293**	**241**	**305**	**0**	**54.86**
3.	Pakistan	312	96	82	134	0	53.41
4.	West Indies	423	149	130	143	1	53.21
5.	South Africa	303	99	106	98	0	48.29
6.	Sri Lanka	153	41	58	54	0	41.41
7.	India	387	84	127	175	1	39.81
8.	New Zealand	324	59	128	37	0	31.55
9.	Zimbabwe	83	8	49	26	0	14.04
10.	Bangladesh	40	1	35	4	0	2.78

* The win percentage excludes draws and tied matches.

⟿ COWDREY COURAGE ⟿

In England's second innings in the second Test against the West Indies at Lord's in 1963, Colin Cowdrey fractured his left arm when he was struck by a ball from fast bowler Wes Hall. When the ninth wicket fell, however, Cowdrey returned to the wicket, his arm encased in plaster, prepared to bat one-handed if necessary, and watched from the non-striker's end as David Allen played out the last two balls for the tensest of draws.

⟿ FIRST CENTURY OF THE 20th CENTURY ⟿

England's Archie MacLaren recorded the first century-plus score of the twentieth century when he scored 116 against Australia in Sydney on 13 December 1901.[†]

[†] In all Tests, a total of 2,327 Test centuries were scored in the twentieth century.

III

⟶ THE GREAT TEST MATCHES (1) ⟵

James Lillywhite and Alfred Shaw took an England team to visit Australia in 1877, just three years after W.G. Grace's All England XI had been soundly beaten by Eighteen of Victoria on their tour of Australia. However, England's leading batsmen – Grace, Richard Daft and Arthur Shrewsbury – did not undertake this tour. The first match of the 1876–77 series was played at the Melbourne Cricket Ground from 15 to 19 March 1877. Although the idea of the Ashes was some years away, this is considered to be the first ever Test match.

The tour started badly for England when they lost their wicket-keeper, Surrey's Ted Pooley, who was arrested in New Zealand. Pooley was infamous for placing bets with the locals wherever England played and wagering that he could predict the score of all 22 batsmen in a match. On this particular occasion, a New Zealand spectator offered Pooley odds of 20/1, which Pooley took at one shilling per player. Pooley then wrote down on a piece of paper that all 22 batsmen would score 0, since being out for a duck has always been the most common score in cricket. As it turned out, 11 batsmen were out for nought, thus winning Pooley £11, less the 11 shillings he lost on those players who scored at least one run. When the spectator refused to pay Pooley, a fight ensued and Pooley was arrested. When the first Test began, he was awaiting trial. As England's squad comprised only 12 players, opening batsman John Selby was asked to keep wicket.

Australia won the toss for this timeless match and opted to bat. England and Alfred Shaw bowled the first ever ball in Test cricket to Australia's Charles Bannerman. Five of the Australian side were English-born, including their highest run-scorer, Bannerman who retired hurt after scoring 165, the first Test century, and their best bowlers, W.E. Midwinter, who took 5–78 in the first innings, and Tom Kendall, 7–55 in the second. In their first innings the Aussies were all out for 245; England replied with 196 all out, Harry Jupp top-scoring with 63. Shaw took 5–38 as Australia were bowled out for only 104 in their second innings, so England had a target of 154 runs to win. However, Andrew Greenwood was out second ball, without scoring, and despite Selby scoring 38, England were dismissed for 108 to hand the Aussies a 45-run victory. In mitigation, England were hampered because half the team suffered from stomach upsets following their boat journey from New Zealand to Australia.

Did You Know That?

Billy Midwinter also played for England, and is the only cricketer to have played for England in Australia and for Australia in England.

Ⅲ

AUSTRALIA V ENGLAND – First Test

15–19 MARCH 1877, MELBOURNE CRICKET GROUND, AUSTRALIA

Result: Australia won by 45 runs. *Toss:* Australia. *Umpires:* CA Reid and RB Terry

AUSTRALIA

Batsman	First Innings		Runs	Second Innings		Runs
C Bannerman	retired hurt		165		b Ulyett	4
NFD Thomson		b Hill	1	c Emmett	b Shaw	7
TP Horan	c Hill	b Shaw	12	c Selby	b Hill	20
*DW Gregory	run out		1	(9)	b Shaw	3
BB Cooper		b Southerton	15		b Shaw	3
WE Midwinter	c Ulyett	b Southerton	5	c Southerton	b Ulyett	17
EJ Gregory	c Greenwood	b Lillywhite	0	c Emmett	b Ulyett	11
†JM Blackham		b Southerton	17	lbw	b Shaw	6
TW Garrett		not out	18	(4) c Emmett	b Shaw	0
TK Kendall	c Southerton	b Shaw	3		not out	17
JR Hodges		b Shaw	0		b Lillywhite	8
Extras	(b 4, lb 2, w 2)		8	(b 5, lb 3)		8
TOTAL	(all out)		245	(all out)		104

1/2, 2/40, 3/41, 4/118, 5/142,
6/143, 7/197, 8/243, 9/245

1/7, 2/27, 3/31, 4/31, 5/35,
6/58, 7/71, 8/75, 9/75, 10/104

Bowling:*First Innings* Shaw–55.3–34–51–3, Hill–23–10–42–1, Ulyett–25–12–36–0, Southerton–37–17–61–3, Armitage–3–0–15–0 (2w), Lillywhite–14–5–19–1, Emmett–12–7–13–0.
Second Innings Shaw–34–16–38–5, Ulyett–19–7–39–3, Hill–14–6–18–1, Lillywhite–1–0–1–1.

ENGLAND

Batsman	First Innings		Runs	Second Innings		Runs
H Jupp	lbw	b Garrett	63	(3) lbw	b Midwinter	4
†J Selby	c Cooper	b Hodges	7	(5) c Horan	b Hodges	38
HRJ Charlwood	c Blackham	b Midwinter	36	(4)	b Kendall	13
G Ulyett	lbw	b Thomson	10	(6)	b Kendall	24
A Greenwood	c EJ Gregory	b Midwinter	1	(2) c Midwinter	b Kendall	5
T Armitage	c Blackham	b Midwinter	9	(8) c Blackham	b Kendall	3
A Shaw		b Midwinter	10	st Blackham	b Kendall	2
T Emmett		b Midwinter	8	(9)	b Kendall	9
A Hill	not out		35	(1) c Thomson	b Kendall	0
*J Lillywhite Jr	c & b	Kendall	10		b Hodges	4
J Southerton	c Cooper	b Garrett	6		not out	1
Extras	(lb 1)		1	(b 4, lb 1)		5
TOTAL	(all out)		196	(all out)		108

1/23, 2/79, 3/98, 4/109, 5/121
6/135, 7/145, 8/145, 9/168, 10/196

1/0, 2/7, 3/20, 4/22, 5/62
6/68, 7/92, 8/93, 9/100, 10/108

Bowling: *First Innings* Hodges–9–0–27–1, Garrett–18.1–10–22–2, Kendall–38–16–54–1, Midwinter–54–23–78–5, Thomson–17–10–14–1. *Second Innings* Kendall–33.1–12–55–7, Midwinter–19–7–23–1, DW Gregory–5–1–9–0, Garrett–2–0–9–0, Hodges–7–5–7–2.

II

❧ BARNES GETS IT IN THE RIBS ❧

During his second tour of England in 1948, the Australian batsman Sid Barnes was heavily criticized for his decision to field a mere five yards from the bat. However, England's Dick Pollard made Barnes think twice about his choice when he struck him in the ribs with a full-blooded pull-drive in the third Test match at Old Trafford. Barnes ended up in hospital for ten days, and after the tour finished he dropped out of cricket for two years to concentrate on a career as a journalist, often writing highly outspoken articles.

❧ TOP 5 GREATEST INNINGS-WIN MARGINS ❧

England holds the record for the greatest innings-win margins. Here are the all-time top five:

Pos.	Margin	Teams	Venue	Year
1.	Innings and 579 runs	England (903-7 d) beat Australia (201 & 123)	The Oval	1938
2.	Innings and 360 runs	Australia (652-7 d) beat South Africa (159 & 133)	Johannesburg	2001/02
3.	Innings and 336 runs	West Indies (614-5 d) beat India (124 & 154)	Kolkata	1958/59
4.	Innings and 332 runs	Australia (645) beat England (141 & 172)	Brisbane	1946/47
5.	Innings and 324 runs	Pakistan (643) beat New Zealand (73 & 246)	Lahore	2002

❧ AN ENGLISH HERO ❧

During the Brisbane Test of the infamous "Bodyline Tour" of Australia in 1932–33, England's Eddie Paynter was taken to hospital suffering from tonsillitis. When, next day, Paynter heard that his team-mates were struggling at 216 for six, in reply to Australia's score of 340, Paynter discharged himself from hospital and came out to bat. He declined the offer of a runner from Aussie skipper Bill Woodfull and scored 83, helping England to what had previously seemed an unlikely first-innings lead. He then fielded for a couple of hours, before retiring to the pavilion. In the second innings England needed 20 to win when Paynter came out to bat and hit the winning runs with a glorious six off McCabe.

[1] *In seven Test matches against Australia, Paynter averaged 84.42, easily the best by an England batsman against the Aussies.*

II

~ MICHAEL ATHERTON, OBE ~

Michael Andrew Atherton was born on 23 March 1968 in Failsworth, Manchester. He made his first-class debut in 1987. Two years later, Atherton, aged just 21, scored more than 1,000 runs, captained Cambridge University, and made his England Test debut. After four years as an opener for his country, Mike was appointed captain in 1993 and led an England side for the first time against Australia at Old Trafford. Atherton went on to captain England a record number of times, 54, without ever gaining the popularity enjoyed by successors such as Michael Vaughan or Andrew Flintoff with the media or fans. However, he was well liked by his Lancashire team-mates and his England colleagues. A gifted leg-break bowler early in his career, he took 6 for 78 against Nottinghamshire in the County Championship in 1990. That same year, Atherton won the Cricket Writers' Club Young Cricketer of the Year Award, and in 1991 he was named as one of *Wisden*'s Cricketers of the Year.

After England's disappointing tour of the West Indies in 1997–98. a tour in which England won one, lost three and drew two of their six Tests, Atherton resigned as England captain. During the 3–1 Test series defeat, he had averaged just 17 runs. Michael had led his country in 52 Tests over four and a half years when he stepped down, England winning 13, losing 19 and drawing 20. He went on to captain England twice more, against Australia in 2001, losing both matches. In a long Test career, Atherton won 115 England caps and scored 7,728 runs at an average of 37.69.

Atherton wasn't England's most stylish batsman, but he was hard to dislodge and became one of the world's best openers. Maybe his finest moment for England came in the second Test against South Africa at the New Wanderers Stadium, Johannesburg, in December 1995, when he battled for 643 minutes to score 185 not out as England chased an improbably target of 479.

In 1997 he was awarded the OBE in recognition of his services to cricket. Throughout his career Mike suffered from back problems, which effectively ended his career as a bowler in the early 1990s and forced him to withdraw from England's 1999 World Cup squad. He played no more one-day internationals, but did return briefly to the England Test side. He retired in 2001, becoming cricket correspondent for the *Daily Telegraph* and a television commentator.

Did You Know That?
Michael Atherton is a huge Manchester United fan, and his father was on their books as a young boy.

❚❚❚

⟿ HONOURS LIST ⟿

The following are just some of the England cricketers to receive an honour from the Queen:

Knighthoods

Sir George Oswald Browning
(Gubby) Allen CBE
Sir Alec Bedser
Sir Colin Cowdrey CBE
Sir Jack Hobbs
Sir Leonard Hutton
Sir Pelham Warner

OBEs

Michael Atherton
Ian Botham
Geoffrey Boycott
Mike Brearley
Basil D'Oliveira
Hugh Bromley-Davenport
Keith Fletcher
Mike Gatting
Graham Gooch
David Gower
Alec Stewart
Micky Stewart
Michael Vaughan

CBEs

Denis Compton
Basil D'Oliveira
Ray Illingworth
Brian Statham

MBEs

Dennis Amiss
Ian Bell
Paul Collingwood
John Edrich
Andrew Flintoff
Ashley Giles
Steve Harmison
Matthew Hoggard
Geraint Jones
Simon Jones
Kevin Pietersen
Andrew Strauss
Graham Thorpe
Marcus Trescothick
Derek Underwood
Bob Willis

Did You Know That?

Colin Cowdrey was appointed CBE in 1972, knighted in 1992 and in 1997 became the first cricketer to be raised to the peerage for his services to cricket.

⟿ THE FIRST TEST ON ENGLISH SOIL ⟿

The first ever Test match on English soil was played at the Kennington Oval, London, on 6 September 1880. England defeated Australia by five wickets, with W.G. Grace scoring a century on his debut. The Oval is where Test series in England traditionally end.[†]

[†] *The Kennington Oval also hosted the first ever FA Cup Final, in which the Wanderers FC beat the Royal Engineers 1–0, and the finals of 1874–92 inclusive.*

Ⅲ

⟶ THE HOME OF CRICKET ⟵

Lord's is regarded throughout the world as the "home of cricket" and the game's spiritual headquarters. Lord's is owned by the Marylebone Cricket Club (MCC), which to this day is the guardian of both the laws of the game and the spirit of the game. MCC sides promote cricket worldwide by playing in excess of 450 games each year, both in Britain and abroad. Lord's is also the home of Middlesex County Cricket Club, the England & Wales Cricket Board (ECB) and the European Cricket Council (ECC). In addition to Test matches, Lord's hosts one-day internationals, most of Middlesex's home games, some historic fixtures, including Eton v Harrow and the Varsity Match, and a number of village and club cricket finals. Lord's is also the setting for the state-of-the-art MCC Indoor School, the MCC Library and the famous MCC Museum, where exhibits include the Ashes urn and the Wisden Trophy.

⟶ TOP FIVE TEST BOWLING RETURNS ⟵

Three England bowlers occupy places in the top five of the table for the most impressive bowling figures in an innings:

Pos.	Bowling	Player	Match	Venue	Year
1.	10–53	Jim Laker (ENG)	England v Australia	Manchester	1956
2.	10–74	Anil Kumble (IND)	India v Pakistan	Delhi	1998–99
3.	9–28	George Lohmann (ENG)	England v South Africa	Johannesburg	1895–96
4.	9–37	Jim Laker (ENG)	England v Australia	Manchester	1956
5.	9–51	Muttiah Muralitharan (SL)	Sri Lanka v Zimbabwe	Kandy	2001–02

⟶ THE FULL MONTY ⟵

Mudhsuden Singh Panesar, "Monty" for short, became the first Sikh to play for England when he appeared against India at Nagpur in the first Test of the 2005–06 tour. Panesar was one of three England debutants in the drawn match, along with Ian Blackwell and Alastair Cook.[†]

[†] *Monty Panesar was born and raised in Luton, but his grandparents still live in the Indian industrial city of Ludhiana, known as the "Manchester of the East".*

⫼

↬ ASHES FEVER (2) ↫

"I'm going to have a stinking hangover. They said when we won the Ashes it would be life-changing, and I think we had a small taste of it. We're going to enjoy it."
Andrew Flintoff gets ready to celebrate on the Monday night after the 2005 Ashes were won

↬ BLACKWELL RECEIVES THE CALL ↫

On 7 February 2006, England called up Somerset left-arm spinner Ian Blackwell after Warwickshire left-arm spinner Ashley Giles failed to recover from hip surgery in time to fly out with the England squad to tour India in February/March 2006. However, a replacement was not called up for Blackwell to the England A squad who were touring the Caribbean at the time. Blackwell, who had already played in 28 one-day internationals for England, made his Test debut at Nagpur on 1 March 2006. Blackwell bowled 19 overs, without taking a wicket, and scored four runs in the drawn match.

↬ OCCUPYING THE CREASE ↫

Only five players in history have batted on all five days of a Test match, with two Englishman achieving the remarkable feat. Geoffrey Boycott did it in 1977 against Australia when he opened at the close of the first day, hit a century in the first innings over the next two days and then got back into bat at the end of day four before steering England to victory with 80 not out. Allan Lamb did the same against West Indies in 1984 with a dogged 110 over three days in the second innings, although England ultimately lost.

Name	Country	1st inns	2nd inns	Opp.	Venue	Year
M Jaisimha	Ind	20*	74	Aus	Calcutta	1959–60
G Boycott	Eng	107	80*	Aus	Nottingham	1977
KJ Hughes	Aus	117	84	Eng	Lords	1980
AJ Lamb	Eng	23	110	WI	Lords	1984
RJ Shastri	Ind	111	7*	Eng	Calcutta	1984–85

↬ THE CENTURION MILLENNIUM MAN ↫

Ian Botham achieved the double of 1,000 runs and 100 wickets in the least number of Test matches. He reached the landmark in his 21st Test.

III

⚬ FANTASY ENGLAND XI (2) ⚬

DURHAM

1	*Colin* MILBURN*
2	*Graham* FOWLER* *(WICKET-KEEPER)*
3	*John* MORRIS*
4	*Wayne* LARKINS*
5	*Ian* BOTHAM*
6	*Gary* PRATT**
7	*Paul* COLLINGWOOD
8	*David* GRAVENEY* *(CAPTAIN)*
9	*Liam* PLUNKETT
10	*Steve* HARMISON
11	*Simon* BROWN
12th Man	*Geoff* COOK*

All played for England, but
* Not as Durham players
** As a substitute fielder – Ashes 2005

Did You Know That?

Durham CCC is English cricket's youngest first-class county, having been granted first-class status in 1992. Durham's county ground, the Riverside, is also England's newest Test match ground[†], hosting its first Test in June 2003, when England played Zimbabwe. Durham are one of only four counties never to have won the County Championship.

⚬ TOP 5 TEST BATTING AVERAGES ⚬

English players are fourth and fifth in the list of those who have recorded the highest batting averages during their Test careers (a minimum of 20 innings required):

Pos.	Average	Player	Period
1.	99.94	Don Bradman (AUS)	from 1928 to 1948
2.	60.97	Graeme Pollock (SA)	from 1963 to 1970
3.	60.83	George Headley (WI)	from 1930 to 1954
4.	60.73	Herbert Sutcliffe (ENG)	from 1924 to 1935
5.	59.23	Eddie Paynter (ENG)	from 1931 to 1939

[†]*Cardiff's Sophia Gardens will host a Test match when Australia next tour England in 2009.*

III

~ TOP 5 WINNING MARGINS BY RUNS ~

England holds the record for the greatest winning margin in Tests in terms of runs. Here are the all-time top five:

Pos.	Margin	Teams	Venue	Year
1.	675 runs	England (521 & 342–8 d) beat Australia (122 & 66)	Brisbane Exhibition Grd	1928–29
2.	562 runs	Australia (701 & 327) beat England (321 & 145)	The Oval, London	1934
3.	530 runs	Australia (328 & 578) beat South Africa (205 & 171)	Melbourne	1910–11
4.	491 runs	Australia (381 & 361–5 d) beat Pakistan (179 & 72)	Perth	2004–05
5.	425 runs	West Indies (211 & 411–5 d) beat England (71 & 126)	Manchester	1976

~ QUIETLY GOES THE DON ~

On the occasion of his last international innings, Don Bradman needed just four runs to be able to retire with a Test batting average of 100, but he was dismissed without scoring by England spin bowler Eric Hollies. Bradman, having been applauded on to the pitch by both teams, it was sometimes claimed that he was unable to see the ball due to the tears welling in his eyes, a claim the Don always dismissed as sentimental nonsense. Regardless, he was given a guard of honour by players and spectators alike as he left the ground with a batting average of 99.94 from his 52 Tests, nearly double the average of any other player before or since. His average is allegedly immortalized as the post office box number of the Australian Broadcasting Corporation.

~ MOST CONSECUTIVE TEST VICTORIES ~

England lies joint fifth in the table for the most consecutive Test match victories, with eight in 2004 and 2004–05:

Pos.	Wins	Team	Period
1.	16 matches	Australia	from 1999–2000 to 2000–01
2.	11 matches	West Indies	from 1983–84 to 1984–85
=3.	9 matches	South Africa	from 2001–02 to 2003
=3.	9 matches	Sri Lanka	from 2001 to 2001–02
=5.	8 matches	Australia	from 1920–21 to 1921
=5.	8 matches	England	from 2004 to 2004–05

III

⌒ FAMOUS "ENDS" AT ENGLISH GROUNDS ⌒

The Oval	*Lord's*	*Edgbaston*
Pavilion End	Pavilion End	City End
Vauxhall End	Nursery End	Pavilion End

Old Trafford	*Trent Bridge*	*Riverside*
Stretford End	Pavilion End	Finchale End
Brian Statham	Radcliffe Road	Lumley End

Headingley
Kirkstall Lane
Football Stand

⌒ TEST MATCHES WON BY ONE WICKET ⌒

England was the first country to win a Test match by one wicket. Here is the full list of one-wicket Test victories:

Teams	Venue	Year
England (183 & 263–9) beat Australia (324 & 121)	The Oval, London	1902
South Africa (91 & 287–9) beat England (184 & 190)	Johannesburg	1905–06
England (382 & 282–9) beat Australia (266 & 397)	Melbourne	1907–08
England (183 & 173–9) beat South Africa (113 & 242)	Cape Town	1922/23
Australia (216 & 260–9) beat West Indies (272 & 203)	Melbourne	1951–52
New Zealand (249 & 104–9) beat West Indies (140 & 212)	Dunedin	1979–80
Pakistan (256 & 315–9) beat Australia (337 & 232)	Karachi	1994–95
West Indies (329 & 311–9) beatAustralia (490 & 146)	Bridgetown	1998–99
West Indies (273 & 216–9) beat Pakistan (269 & 219)	St John's	1999–2000
Pakistan (175 & 262–9) beat Bangladesh (281 & 154)	Multan	2003

Did You Know That?
The Oval's famous gasholders are situated at the Vauxhall End.

Ⅲ

⚮ THE GREAT TEST MATCHES (2) ⚮

The fourth Test of the 1928–29 Ashes series was played at the Adelaide Oval, Australia, from 1 to 8 February 1929. This was a true epic Ashes battle in every sense, with some particularly outstanding individual performances. The 17-strong England party that toured Australia that year included four batsmen in their twenties: the captain, Percy Chapman, and Douglas Jardine, both amateurs, and Wally Hammond and Morris Leyland, both professionals.

Unusually, the Adelaide Test of 1928–29 was the fourth Test of the series – it was normally the third – and it had been preceded by Brisbane's first ever Test, at the Exhibition Ground, and Tests in Sydney and Melbourne. In order to foster good sportsmanship between the opposing teams, the English sweet manufacturer John Mackintosh & Sons Limited sent gifts to every player and official of the England and Australia sides prior to the game with the message: "Convey to members of English and Australian Elevens our best wishes for a pleasant and closely-fought match, and give each a small piece of our toffee as a reminder that we are taking a keen interest in the game". The friendliness of the 1928–29 tour was turned on its head four years later during England's famous Bodyline tour.

England won the toss in the 1929 Adelaide Test, a timeless match, and chose to bat. In their first innings the tourists' openers Jack Hobbs and Herbert Sutcliffe put on 143 for the first wicket and Wally Hammond scored an unbeaten 119, but England were still bowled out for 334. Australia lost three wickets for 19 runs before Scottish-born Archie Jackson, aged just 19, led the recovery with 164 and they replied with 369 all out. In their second innings, England lost both openers before they had wiped out their first-innings deficit, but 98 from Jardine and 177 from Hammond righted the ship. Maurice Tate scored 47 to help England finish up 383 all out, thereby setting Australia 349 runs to win. Six out of Australia's top seven batsmen reached 20 – Ted Hendry, with five, missed out – but none could make it to three figures. The crucial wicket was Don Bradman's run out when on 58, and the Aussies were finally bowled out for 336, so England won the match by 12 runs.

Somerset's left-arm spinner, Jack "Farmer" White, who was on his only Australian tour at the age of 37, took 13 for 256 from 124.5 overs, including eight for 126 in the second innings. Such was the impact that White had on the series that former Australian captain Monty Noble declared: "White was the only man who truly and actually won the Ashes". Tragically, Australia's leading batsman in the Test, Jackson, was to die of tuberculosis just four years later.

AUSTRALIA V ENGLAND – Fourth Test
1–8 FEBRUARY 1929, ADELAIDE OVAL, AUSTRALIA

Result: England won by 12 runs. *Toss:* England. *Umpires:* DA Elder, GA Hele.

ENGLAND

Batsman	Dismissal 1st	Bowler 1st	Runs 1st	Dismissal 2nd	Bowler 2nd	Runs 2nd
JB Hobbs	c Ryder	b Hendry	74	c Oldfield	b Hendry	1
H Sutcliffe	st Oldfield	b Grimmett	64	c Oldfield	b a'Beckett	17
WR Hammond	not out		119	c & b	Ryder	177
DR Jardine	lbw	b Grimmett	1	c Woodfull	b Oxenham	98
EH Hendren		b Blackie	13	c Bradman	b Blackie	11
*APF Chapman	c a'Beckett	b Ryder	39	c Woodfull	b Blackie	0
†G Duckworth	c Ryder	b Grimmett	5	(11) lbw	b Oxenham	1
H Larwood		b Hendry	3	(7) lbw	b Oxenham	5
G Geary	run out		3	(8) c & b	Grimmett	6
MW Tate		b Grimmett	2	(9) lbw	b Oxenham	47
JC White	c Ryder	b Grimmett	0	(10) not out		4
Extras	(b 3, lb 7, w 1)		11	(b 6, lb 10)		16
TOTAL	(all out)		334	(all out)		383

1/143, 2/143, 3/149, 4/179, 5/246, 6/263, 7/270, 8/308, 9/312, 10/334

1/1, 2/21, 3/283, 4/296, 5/297, 6/302, 7/327, 8/337, 9/381, 10/383

Bowling: *First Innings:* a'Beckett 31–8–44–0, Hendry 31–14–49–2, Grimmett 52.1–12–102–5, Oxenham 35–14–51–0, Blackie 29–6–57–1, Ryder 5–1–20–1; *Second Innings:* a'Beckett 27–9–41–1, Hendry 28–11–56–1, Grimmett 52–15–117–1, Oxenham 47.4–21–67–4, Blackie 39–11–70–2, Ryder 5–1–13–1, Kippax 2–0–3–0.

AUSTRALIA

Batsman	Dismissal 1st	Bowler 1st	Runs 1st	Dismissal 2nd	Bowler 2nd	Runs 2nd
WM Woodfull	c Duckworth	b Tate	1	c Geary	b White	30
A Jackson	lbw	b White	164	c Duckworth	b Geary	36
HSTL Hendry	c Duckworth	b Larwood	2	c Tate	b White	5
AF Kippax		b White	3	c Hendren	b White	51
*J Ryder	lbw	b White	63	c & b	White	87
DG Bradman	c Larwood	b Tate	40	run out		58
EL a'Beckett	hit wicket	b White	36	c Hammond	b White	21
RK Oxenham	c Chapman	b White	15	c Chapman	b White	12
†WAS Oldfield		b Tate	32	not out		15
CV Grimmett		b Tate	4	c Tate	b White	9
DD Blackie	not out		3	c Larwood	b White	0
Extras	(lb 5, w 1)		6	(b 9, lb 3)		12
TOTAL	(all out)		369	(all out)		336

1/1, 2/6, 3/19, 4/145, 5/227, 6/287, 7/323, 8/336, 9/365, 10/369

1/65, 2/71, 3/74, 4/211, 5/224, 6/258, 7/308, 8/320, 9/336, 10/336

Bowling: *First Innings:* Larwood 37–6–92–1, Tate 42–10–77–4, White 60–16–130–5, Geary 12–3–32–0, Hammond 9–1–32–0. *Second Innings:* Larwood 20–4–60–0, Tate 37–9–75–0, White 64.5–21–126–8, Geary 16–2–42–1, Hammond 14–3–21–0.

Ⅲ

↝ CAPTAINS OF ENGLAND ↜

Players who captained England in one Test match

Name	Counties	Seasons	Matches
CA Smith	Sussex	1888/89	1
MP Bowden	Surrey	1888/89	1
TC O'Brien	Middlesex	1895/96	1
GTS Stevens	Middlesex	1927/28	1
CF Walters	Glamorgan	1934	1
K Cranston	Lancashire	1947/48	1
DB Carr	Derbyshire	1951/52	1
TW Graveney	Gloucestershire, Worcestershire	1968	1
JH Edrich	Surrey	1974/75	1
CS Cowdrey	Kent, Glamorgan	1988	1
MA Butcher	Surrey	1999	1

Players who captained England between 2 and 5 Tests

Name	Counties	Seasons	Matches
FS Jackson	Yorkshire	1905	5
FL Fane	Essex	1907/08–1909/10	5
FT Mann	Middlesex	1922/23	5
Lord Harris	Kent	1878/79–1884	4
A Shaw	Nottinghamshire, Sussex	1881/82	4
IFW Bligh	Kent	1882/83	4
AG Steel	Lancashire	1886–1888	4
Lord Hawke	Yorkshire	1895/96–1898/99	4
RT Stanyforth	Yorkshire	1927/28	4
JC White	Somerset	1928/29– 1929	4
AHH Gilligan	Sussex	1929/30	4
FSG Calthorpe	Sussex, Warwickshire	1929/30	4
ND Howard	Lancashire	1951/52	4
G Boycott	Yorkshire	1977/78	4
RE Foster	Worcestershire	1907	3
HDG Leveson-Gower	Surrey	1909/10	3
Lord Tennyson	Hampshire	1921	3
RWV Robins	Middlesex	1937	3
AJ Lamb	Northamptonshire	1989/90–1990/91	3
J Lillywhite	Sussex	1876/77	2
AN Hornby	Lancashire	1882–1884	2
WW Read	Surrey	1887/88–1891/92	2

AO Jones	Nottinghamshire)	1907/08	2
DS Sheppard	Sussex)	1954	2
JE Emburey	Middlesex,	1988	2
	Northamptonshire)		
ME Trescothick	Somerset)	2004/05	2

Players who captained England between 6 and 10 Tests

Name	Counties	Seasons	Matches
PF Warner	Middlesex	1903/04–1905/06	10
AER Gilligan	Surrey, Sussex	1924–1924/25	9
AE Stoddart	Middlesex	1893–1897/98	8
AR Lewis	Glamorgan	1972/73	8
A Shrewsbury	Nottinghamshire	1884/85–1886/87	7
FG Mann	Middlesex	1948/49–1949	7
DB Close	Yorkshire,	1966–1967	7
	Somerset		
KWR Fletcher	Essex	1981/82	7
CB Fry	Hampshire,	1912	6
	Sussex		
AW Carr	Nottinghamshire	1926–1929	6
A Flintoff	Lancashire	2005/06–06	6

Players who captained England between 11 and 20 Tests

Name	Counties	Seasons	Matches
WR Hammond	Gloucestershire	1938–1946/47	20
MH Denness	Kent, Essex	1973/74–1975	19
JWHT Douglas	Essex	1911/12–1924	18
RGD Willis	Surrey,	1982–1983/84	18
	Warwickshire		
APF Chapman	Kent	1926–1930/31	17
RES Wyatt	Warwickshire	1930–1935	16
DR Jardine	Surrey	1931–1933/34	15
FR Brown	Surrey,	1949–1951	15
	Northamptonshire		
AJ Stewart	Surrey	1992/93–2001	15
NWD Yardley	Yorkshire	1946/47–1950	14
AW Greig	Sussex	1975–1976/77	14
WG Grace	Gloucestershire,	1888–1899	13
	Kent		
IT Botham	Somerset,	1980–1981	12
	Worcestershire, Durham		
GOB Allen	Middlesex	1936–1947/48	11

Players who captained England in more than 20 Tests

Name	Counties	Seasons	Matches
MA Atherton	Lancashire	1993–2001	54
N Hussain	Essex	1999–2003	45
PBH May	Surrey	1955–1961	41
GA Gooch	Essex	1988–1993	34
MP Vaughan	Yorkshire	2003–2005	33*
DI Gower	Leicestershire, Hampshire	1982–1989	32
R Illingworth	Yorkshire, Leicestershire	1969–1973	31
JM Brearley	Middlesex	1977–1981	31
ER Dexter	Sussex	1961/62–1964	30
MC Cowdrey	Kent	1959– 1968/69	27
MJK Smith	Warwickshire, Leicestershire	1963/64–1966	25
L Hutton	Yorkshire	1952–1954/55	23
MW Gatting	Middlesex	1986–1988	23
AC MacLaren	Lancashire	1897/98–1909	22

*Current England captain (figures up to the end of the 2006 Test series against Sri Lanka)

⟋ BABY FLINTOFF ⟍

Andrew Flintoff, the England captain, went into the second Test against India after learning that his wife Rachael had given birth to their second child, a boy, Corey. The baby had been due to be born around 21 March 2006, and Freddie originally made plans to miss the Third Test, to be at Rachael's side for the birth. However, he decided to stay in India after being named England captain ahead of the first Test following an injury to Michael Vaughan. England tied the series 1–1 after bowling India out for 100 in their second innings to clinch a dramatic victory in the final Test at Mumbai.

⟋ ALEC THE GREAT ⟍

Alec Stewart is England's most-capped Test cricketer, having played in 133 matches between 1990 and 2003. (The world record is held by Australia's Steve Waugh, who played 168 Tests between 1985 and 2004.) Stewart also holds four other England records: the most dismissals in Test cricket (277, inc. 36 catches as a fielder); the most dismissals in ODIs (174, inc. 11 catches as a fielder); the highest number of ODIs played (170); and the most runs in ODIs (4,677).

III

⟿ FANTASY ENGLAND XI (3) ⟿

ESSEX

1	*Graham* GOOCH *(CAPTAIN)*
2	*Nasser* HUSSAIN
3	*Keith* FLETCHER
4	*Barry* KNIGHT
5	*Trevor* BAILEY
6	*Derek* PRINGLE
7	*James* FOSTER *(WICKET-KEEPER)*
8	*John* LEVER
9	*Ken* FARNES
10	*Peter* SUCH
11	*Neil* FOSTER
12th MAN	*John* CHILDS

Did You Know That?

Essex CCC joined the County Championship in 1895 with three others, Derbyshire, Hampshire and Warwickshire. Essex have won the County Championship seven times (1979, 1983, 1984, 1986, 1991 and 1992). In 2002, they won the Second Division County Championship.

⟿ ASHES FEVER (3) ⟿

"I definitely believe if any of our batsmen get out to Ashley Giles in the Tests they should go and hang themselves. But I am confident that won't happen."
Terry Alderman, *previewing the 2005 Ashes. Giles dismissed all of the top eight Aussie batsmen at least once in the series.*

⟿ ASHES GONGS AROUSE LIVERPUDLIAN IRE ⟿

Liverpool FC voiced their displeasure after the entire England cricket team was honoured in the 2006 New Year's Honours List after winning back the Ashes from Australia. Liverpool pointed out that home-grown UEFA Champions League winners Jamie Carragher and Steven Gerrard were overlooked whilst Paul Collingwood, who only played in one Ashes match, scoring just 17 runs without taking any wickets, was awarded an MBE.

III

⟿ SIR ALEC BEDSER ⟿

Alec Bedser was born on 4 July 1918 in Reading, Berkshire. He arrived minutes after his identical twin brother, Eric. His father was stationed in Reading with the Royal Air Force, but the family moved to Woking when the twins were six months old. Alec and Eric played their first organized cricket aged seven, and over the next decade they played together for Monument Hill School and Woking Cricket Club. When they left school the twins joined a local firm of solicitors, but it wasn't long before their cricket talents were spotted. In 1938 Alan Peach, the Surrey coach, watched the twins practising in the nets for Woking and immediately recruited them to the staff at The Oval. Within a year both made their first-class debuts. However, when World War II broke out in 1939, Alec and Eric were called up by the RAF, and saw action at Dunkirk and in North Africa, Italy and Austria. Alec was impressive in wartime cricket: representing the RAF, he took 6 for 27, including a hat-trick, against the West Indians and 9 for 36 against a Metropolitan Police team, claiming another hat-trick.

Alec was a first-choice in the Surrey side from the start of the 1946 season and made his Test debut against India at Lord's in June of the same year. It was his 13th first-class match and he was 28 years old. He took 11 wickets in each of his first two Tests (11 for 139 in his debut and 11 for 96 in the next game at Old Trafford). In 1947 Bedser was selected as a *Wisden* Cricketer of the Year. Up until 1954 he was the fulcrum of England's attack. In 1953, aged 35, he was instrumental in England's Ashes victory, taking 39 wickets at an average of 17.48, including 14 for 99 at Trent Bridge. Alec played in 51 Tests from 1946 to 1955, and took 236 wickets at 24.89.

Alec took 100 wickets in a season 11 times, and was a key player in Surrey's eight County Championship wins between 1950 and 1958. An outstanding right-arm fast-medium bowler, his first-class career spanned 21 years, during which he took 1,924 first-class wickets in 485 matches. He took five or more wickets in an innings 96 times and ten wickets or more in a match on 16 occasions. A lower-order batsman, he was often took on the role of nightwatchman, but his only first-class century, 126 against Somerset at Taunton in 1947, came batting at number nine. In his final first-class game in 1960, Alec Bedser took 5 for 25 against Glamorgan at his beloved Oval.

After his retirement he stayed in cricket: he served as an England selector for a record 23 years; he was chairman of the selectors between 1969 and 1981; and he also managed England on two overseas tours. In 1996 he was knighted, and the following year he was honoured with the presidency of Surrey CCC.

III

‍⌒ ASHES HISTORY ⌒‍

1882	Eng 0-1 **Aus**
1882/83	Aus 1-2 **Eng**
1884	**Eng** 1-0 Aus
1884/85	Aus 2-3 **Eng**
1886	**Eng** 3-0 Aus
1886/87	Aus 0-2 **Eng**
1887/88	Aus 0-1 **Eng**
1888	**Eng** 2-1 Aus
1890	**Eng** 2-0 Aus
1891/92	**Aus** 2-1 Eng
1893	**Eng** 1-0 Aus
1894/95	Aus 2-3 **Eng**
1896	**Eng** 2-1 Aus
1897/98	**Aus** 4-1 Eng
1899	Eng 0-1 **Aus**
1901/02	**Aus** 4-1 Eng
1903/04	Aus 2-3 **Eng**
1905	**Eng** 2-0 Aus
1907/08	**Aus** 4-1 Eng
1909	Eng 1-2 **Aus**
1911/12	Aus 1-4 **Eng**
1912	**Eng** 1-0 Aus
1920/21	**Aus** 5-0 Eng
1921	Eng 0-3 **Aus**
1924/25	**Aus** 4-1 Eng
1926	**Eng** 1-0 Aus
1928/29	Aus 1-4 **Eng**
1930	Eng 1-2 **Aus**
1932/33	Aus 1-4 **Eng**
1934	Eng 1-2 **Aus**
1936/37	**Aus** 3-2 Eng
1938	Eng 1-1 Aus

1946/47	**Aus** 3-0 Eng
1948	Eng 0-4 **Aus**
1950/51	**Aus** 4-1 Eng
1953	**Eng** 1-0 Aus
1954/55	Aus 1-3 **Eng**
1956	**Eng** 2-1 Aus
1958/59	**Aus** 4-0 Eng
1961	Eng 1-2 **Aus**
1962/63	Aus 1-1 Eng
1964	Eng 0-1 **Aus**
1965/66	Aus 1-1 Eng
1968	Eng 1-1 Aus
1970/71	Aus 0-2 **Eng**
1972	Eng 2-2 Aus
1974/75	**Aus** 4-1 Eng
1975	Eng 0-1 **Aus**
1977	**Eng** 3-0 Aus
1978/79	Aus 1-5 **Eng**
1981	**Eng** 3-1 Aus
1982/83	**Aus** 2-1 Eng
1985	**Eng** 3-1 Aus
1986/87	Aus 1-2 **Eng**
1989	Eng 0-4 **Aus**
1990/91	**Aus** 3-0 Eng
1993	Eng 1-4 **Aus**
1994/95	**Aus** 3-1 Eng
1997	Eng 2-3 **Aus**
1998/99	**Aus** 3-1 Eng
2001	Eng 1-4 **Aus**
2002/03	**Aus** 4-1 Eng
2005	**Eng** 2-1 Aus

‍⌒ THE GENERATION GAME ⌒‍

England's leading batsman of the late 1940s and early 1950s was Denis Compton and his captain when the Ashes were regained in 1953 was Len Hutton. Fast forward some half a century and Middlesex are captained by Ben Hutton, grandson of Len, and one of their bright prospects is Nick Compton, grandson of Denis.

III

⟶ DEFEAT FROM THE JAWS OF VICTORY ⟶

Australia hold the record in Tests for the lowest fourth-innings target successfully defended. England needed 85 runs to beat Australia at The Oval in 1882, but were dramatically bowled out for 77, giving Australia an unlikely seven-run win.

⟶ ENGLAND'S ODI EMBARRASSMENTS ⟶

The highest innings totals against England in one-day international cricket are:

Total	Overs	RPO	For	Venue	Date	Result/England
353–6	50	7.06	Pakistan	Karachi	15.12.2005	(l) by 165 runs
326–8	49.3	6.59	India	Lord's	13.7.2002	(l) by 2 wkts
323–5	50	6.46	Pakistan	Sharjah	7.4.1999	(l) by 90 runs
318–6	50	6.36	Australia	Melbourne	15.12.2002	(l) by 89 runs
313–6	50	6.26	W Indies	Arnos Vale	2.3.1994	(l) by 165 runs
311–7	50	6.22	S Africa	East London	9.2.2005	(l) by 7 runs
304–9	50	6.08	Pakistan	Karachi	24.10.2000	(w) by 5 wkts
303–9	49.4	6.10	Sri Lanka	Adelaide	23.1.1999	(l) by 1 wkt
302–5	50	6.04	W Indies	Port of Spain	8.4.1998	(l) by 57 runs

The biggest defeats margin suffered by England in terms of runs in one-day international cricket are:

Runs	Opponents	Venue	Date
165	West Indies	Arnos Vale	2.3.1994
165	Pakistan	Karachi	15.12.2005
162	Australia	Melbourne	13.2.1999
155	New Zealand	Wellington	16.2.2002
135	West Indies	Bridgetown	19.3.1986
131	Zimbabwe	Harare	3.1.1997
125	Australia	Manchester	14.6.2001
122	South Africa	The Oval	22.5.1999

⟶ THE FIRST EVER TEST MATCH ⟶

The first ever Test match was played between Australia and England at the Melbourne Cricket Ground, from 15 to 19 March 1877. Australia won by 45 runs. Exactly 100 years later England played at the Melbourne Cricket Ground, to commemorate the centenary. Remarkably, Australia again won by 45 runs!

III

⁓ BARMY ARMY SONG (2) ⁓

IN THE LAND WHERE I WAS BORN
(To the tune of "Yellow Submarine")
In the land where I was born
There were some cricketers
To be adored
They can bowl, and they can bat
So I follow them with my backpack
We all follow the English Cricket Team
The English Cricket Team
The English Cricket Team

⁓ HIGHEST INDIVIDUAL TEST SCORES ⁓

Four English batsmen are all former holders of the record for the highest number of runs in a Test match innings. Here is the progressive list of the highest individual Test scores:

	Runs	Player	Match	Venue	Season
1.	165*	Charles Bannerman	Australia v England**	Melbourne	1876/77
2.	211	Billy Murdoch	Australia v England	The Oval	1884
3.	287	Tip Foster	England v Australia	Sydney	1903/04
4.	325	Andy Sandham	England v West Indies	Kingston	1929/30
5.	334	Don Bradman	Australia v England	Leeds	1930
6.	336*	Wally Hammond	England v New Zealand	Auckland	1932/33
7.	364	Len Hutton	England v Australia	The Oval	1938
8.	365*	Garfield Sobers	West Indies v Pakistan	Kingston	1957/58
9.	375	Brian Lara	West Indies v England	St John's	1993/94
10.	380	Matthew Hayden	Australia v Zimbabwe	Perth	2003/04
11.	400*	Brian Lara	West Indies v England	St John's	2003/04

*Not out **This was the inaugural Test match*

II

⤳ THE GREAT TEST MATCHES (3) ⤳

England's 1938–39 tour of South Africa featured the famous "Timeless Test". England led the series 1–0 and it was decided that the final Test in Durban would be played to a finish. South Africa won the toss and elected to bat, ending the first day on 229 for 2 (Pieter van der Bijl 105 not out and Bruce Mitchell 4 not out). On the second day, England's Reg Perks, making his Test debut, bowled the dangerous van der Bijl for 125 to leave South Africa 274 for 4. After a rest day on Sunday 5 March, South Africa were finally all out on day three for 530, with Dudley Nourse making 103 and Perks claiming 5 for 100 off 40 overs. England, who finished day three on 35 for 1, batted through the fourth day to reach 268 for 7 (Les Ames 82 not out and Doug Wright 5 not out). When play resumed on the fifth day, England could only manage a further 48 runs, being bowled out in their first innings for 316, thanks to Eric Dalton's four wickets for 59 runs, his best Test return.

South Africa started their second innings with a lead of 214 runs and they stretched it to 405 before losing a wicket. But Mitchell (89), Eric Rowan (0) and Van Der Bijl (97) all fell with the score on 191 and they closed the fifth day on 193 for 3. On day six, South Africa added 288 runs to finish on 481 all out, Alan Melville scoring 104. England were thus set an improbable target of 696 runs to win. Starting day seven on 0 for 0, they finished on 253 for 1, with Paul Gibb on 78 and Bill Edrich 107 – Len Hutton was out for 55.

Rain washed out the following day and it was a rest day on the Sunday, so England resumed their innings on day nine, 13 March, effectively the 11th since the start of the Test. Edrich and Gibb were the only two batsmen dismissed, but they scored 219 and 120, respectively, as England finished on 496–3, exactly 200 short of their target. Eddie Paynter and Wally Hammond piled on the runs on day 10, Paynter eventually being dismissed for 75 and Hammond for 140, both falling to Dalton's leg-breaks. England reached 654 for 5, just 42 runs short of their target, when it began to rain. Although there was unlikely to be more than a couple of hours of play remaining, the two captains agreed to abandon the match as a draw. The immediate consequence was that England won the series 1–0

Amazingly time had caught up with them. England's boat home left from Cape Town – in the south-west of the country – on 15 March and they were in Durban, on the east coast. In those days, the only method of transport for that distance was by rail and this journey still took two days. It remains the longest ever Test match ever played and the aggegate of runs scored – 1,981 for 35 wickets from 5,461 balls – is still a record in Tests.

SOUTH AFRICA V ENGLAND – Fourth Test

3–14 MARCH 1939, KINGSMEAD, DURBAN

Result: Draw. *Toss:* South Africa. *Umpires:* RGA Ashman, GL Sickler.

SOUTH AFRICA

*A Melville	hit wkt	b Wright	78	(6)	b Farnes	103
PGV van der Bijl		b Perks	125	c Paynter	b Wright	97
EAB Rowan	lbw	b Perks	33	c Edrich	b Verity	0
B Mitchell		b Wright	11	(1) hit wkt	b Verity	89
AD Nourse		b Perks	103	(4) c Hutton	b Farnes	25
KG Viljoen	c Ames	b Perks	0	(5)	b Perks	74
EL Dalton	c Ames	b Farnes	57	c & b	Wright	21
†RE Grieveson		b Perks	75		b Farnes	39
ACB Langton	c Paynter	b Verity	27	c Hammond	b Farnes	6
ES Newson	c & b	Verity	1		b Wright	3
N Gordon	not out		0	not out		7
Extras	(b 2, lb 12, nb 6)		20	(b 5, lb 8, nb 4)		17
TOTAL	(all out)		530	(all out)		481

1/131, 2/219, 3/236, 4/274, 5/278
6/368, 7/475, 8/522, 9/523, 10/530

1/191, 2/191, 3/191, 4/242, 5/346
6/382, 7/434, 8/450, 9/462, 10/481

Bowling: *First Innings:* Farnes 46–9–108–1, Perks 41–5–100–5, Wright 37–6–142–2, Verity 55.6–14–97–2, Hammond 14–4–34–0, Edrich 9–2–29–0. *Second Innings:* Farnes 22.1–2–74–4, Perks 32–6–99–1, Wright 43–7–146–3, Verity 40–9–87–2, Hammond 9–1–30–0, Edrich 6–1–18–0, Hutton 1–0–10–0.

ENGLAND

L Hutton	run out		38		b Mitchell	55
PA Gibb	c Grieveson	b Newson	4		b Dalton	120
E Paynter	lbw	b Langton	62	c Gordon	b Langton	219
*WR Hammond	st Grieveson	b Dalton	24	st Grieveson	b Dalton	140
†LEG Ames	c Dalton	b Langton	84	c Grieveson	b Gordon	75
WJ Edrich	c Rowan	b Langton	1	not out		17
BH Valentine	st Grieveson	b Dalton	26	not out		4
H Verity		b Dalton	3			
DVP Wright	c Langton	b Dalton	26			
K Farnes		b Newson	20			
RTD Perks	not out		2			
Extras	(b 7, lb 17, w 1, nb 1)		26	(b 8, lb 12, w 1, nb 3)		24
TOTAL	(all out)		316	(for 5 wickets)		654

1/9, 2/64, 3/125, 4/169, 5/171
6/229, 7/245, 8/276, 9/305, 10/316

1/78, 2/358, 3/447, 4/611, 5/650

Bowling: *First Innings:* Newson 25.6–5–58–2, Langton 35–12–71–3, Gordon 37–7–82–0, Mitchell 7–0–20–0, Dalton 13–1–59–4. *Second Innings:* Newson 43–4–91–0, Langton 56–12–132–1, Gordon 55.2–10–174–1, Mitchell 37–4–133–1, Dalton 27–3–100–2.

III

⌐ ASHES FEVER (4) ⌐

"Talent in the conventional sense can only take you so far. You need nous, a willingness to work hard and an understanding of what you can do for the team."

Ashley Giles makes his point after England's nail-biting Edgbaston victory in the 2005 Ashes

⌐ TOP 10 TEST SCORES ⌐

Sir Len Hutton and Wally Hammond are the only England batsmen to appear in the table for top ten highest individual Test innings:

Runs	Player	For	Oppts	Inns	Test	Venue	Year
400*	Brian Lara	West Indies	England	1st	4th	St John's	2004
380	Matthew Hayden	Australia	Zimbabwe	1st	1st	Perth	2003
375	Brian Lara	West Indies	England	1st	5th	St John's	1994
365*	Garfield Sobers	West Indies	Pakistan	1st	3rd	Kingston	1958
364	Len Hutton	England	Australia	1st	5th	The Oval	1938
340	Sanath Jayasuriya	Sri Lanka	India	1st	1st	Colombo	1997
337	Hanif Mohammad	Pakistan	West Indies	2nd	1st	Bridgetown	1958
336*	Wally Hammond	England	New Zealand	1st	2nd	Auckland	1933
334*	Mark Taylor	Australia	Pakistan	1st	2nd	Peshawar	1998
334	Donald Bradman	Australia	England	1st	3rd	Leeds	1930

* Not out

⌐ DON'S UNUSUAL DOUBLE ⌐

The legendary Don Bradman twice scored a century and a duck in a Test match against England. During the 1932/33 season he scored 0 (dismissed first ball) and 103 not out at Melbourne, and in 1948 he scored 138 and 0 at Trent Bridge. The name 'Bradman' is now protected in Australia and cannot be used as part of a trademark.

⌐ FANTASY ENGLAND XI (4) ⌐

GLAMORGAN

1	*Steve* JAMES	
2	*Hugh* MORRIS	
3	*Cyril* WALTERS	
4	*Tony* LEWIS	(CAPTAIN)
5	*Matthew* MAYNARD	
6	*Maurice* TURNBULL	
7	*Eifion* JONES	(WICKET-KEEPER)
8	*Robert* CROFT	
9	*Simon* JONES	
10	*Steve* WATKIN	
11	*Jeff* JONES	
12th Man	*Johnnie* CLAY	

Did You Know That?
During his career Eifion Jones claimed a Glamorgan county record 933 dismissals. His outstanding displays for them almost won him a place on England's Ashes tour in 1970/71. Glamorgan have been County Champions three times (1948, 1969 and 1997), but no Glamorgan wicket-keeper has played for England in a Test match.

⌐ ENGLAND IN EAST PAKISTAN ⌐

The first ever Test match to be played in Dhaka during the East Pakistan (pre Bangladesh) era took place on 1st January 1955 when Pakistan played India in the first Test. The following table shows England's appearances in Dhaka during the East Pakistan period:

19 Jan 1962	Pakistan v England, 2nd Test
28 Feb 1969	Pakistan v England, 2nd Test

⌐ COLLINGWOOD CEMENTS HIS PLACE ⌐

Before Marcus Trescothick and Michael Vaughan returned home prior to the first Test of England's 2006 tour of India, Paul Collingwood had not been guaranteed his place in England's starting line-up. However, after scoring 134 not out in the first Test against India at Nagpur, he cemented his place in the side. The First Test ended in a draw.

Ⅲ

~ THE HONG KONG SIXES ~

The first ever Hong Kong International Cricket Sixes competition was held in 1992. Pakistan won the inaugural tournament, beating India in the final. The Kowloon Cricket Club hosted the competition and remained the host venue until 1996, when the Sixes moved to the Hong Kong International Stadium for two years. The competition was not staged from 1998 to 2000, but it was resurrected in 2001 and returned to its original home, the Kowloon Cricket Club. The winning nation is presented with the beautiful Butani Cup, which was made by Butani Jewellery. It took one month to design and 15 skilled craftsman three months to complete. The trophy weighs 15kg and is hand sculpted from pure silver and dipped in solid 24-carat gold. Valued in excess of HK$300,000, the trophy depicts, at its top, a batsman hitting six cricket balls studded with 12 carats of diamonds and 60 carats of rubies. The six balls represent the Hong Kong Cricket Sixes. The base of the trophy bears cricket helmets made from gold and enamel, with each helmet representing the national colours of all the cricket-playing nations. England and Pakistan have dominated the competition with four wins each. The full roll of honour is as follows:

Year	Winner	Runners Up	Player Of The Tournament
2005	India	West Indies	Reetinder Sodhi (India)*
2004	England	Sri Lanka	Butt Hussain (Hong Kong)*
2003	England	Pakistan	Saman Jayanthe (Sri Lanka)*
2002	Pakistan	England	Deane Hills (Australia)*
2001	Pakistan	South Africa	Wasim Akram (Pakistan)
1997	Pakistan	England	Zahoor Elahi (Pakistan)
1996	West Indies	India	Derek Crookes (South Africa)
1995	South Africa	England	Jonty Rhodes (South Africa)
1994	England	Australia	Robin Smith (England)
1993	England	Sri Lanka	Phil DeFreitas (England)
1992	Pakistan	India	Wasim Akram (Pakistan)

*Since 2002, with the consent of the Hollioake family, the Player of the Tournament has been presented with the Ben Hollioake Trophy in memory of England's Ben Hollioake, who was tragically killed in a road accident in 2002. Ben grew up in Hong Kong and played for England in the Hong Kong Cricket Sixes in 1997 and 2001.

~ SUCH LUCK ~

Peter Such took 6 for 67 in 33.3 overs in Australia's first innings on his Test debut for England at Old Trafford in June 1993.

Ⅲ

❧ 100 RUNS AND 5 WICKETS IN A TEST ❧

Ian Botham achieved the feat of scoring a century and taking five wickets in an innings an incredible six times. When England played India in Bombay in 1980, he scored 114 and took 6 for 58 in the first innings.

❧ CAPTAIN FREDDIE ❧

When Michael Vaughan was forced to fly home with a knee injury prior to England's first Test match against India of their 2005/06 tour, Andrew Flintoff was appointed the stand-in England captain.

❧ MOST CONSECUTIVE TEST DEFEATS ❧

England occupies joint third and joint fifth positions in the table for the highest number of consecutive Test defeats:

Pos.	Losses	Team	Period
1.	21 matches	Bangladesh	from 2001/02 to 2003/04
2.	11 matches	Zimbabwe	from 2001/02 to 2003/04
=3.	8 matches	England	from 1920/21 to 1921
=3.	8 matches	South Africa	from 1888/89 to 1898/99
=5.	7 matches	Australia	from 1884/85 to 1887/88
=5.	7 matches	England	from 1950 to 1950/51
=5.	7 matches	England	from 1985/86 to 1986
=5.	7 matches	England	from 1992 to 1993
=5.	7 matches	India	from 1967 to 1967/68
=5.	7 matches	West Indies	from 2000 to 2000/01

❧ A RECORD YEAR FOR LORD'S TOUR ❧

The excitement and renewed interest in cricket generated by the Ashes series in the summer of 2005 resulted in a record-breaking year for MCC's tours of Lord's. The previous annual record of 29,500 visitors was broken with more than ten weeks of the year remaining. The 2005 monthly visitor figures were approximately 33% higher than 2004. Indeed, from the start of the 2005 Ashes series, the tours attracted more than 4,000 visitors every month. This was the first time since the launch of the tours of Lord's in 1990 that the 4,000 mark had been reached. The tours enable visitors from around the world to see behind the scenes at "the home of cricket", where the key attractions include the recently refurbished pavilion, the award-winning NatWest Media Centre and, of course, the world-famous Ashes urn.

III

⌒ GET EM' OFF! ⌒

18–22 August 1999	A streaker ran on to the pitch and interrupted play during the fourth Test between England and New Zealand at The Oval.
12 December 1999	England's Phil Tufnell walked past a streaker who ran on to the pitch during the fourth day of the second Test between England and South Africa at the St George's Park ground, Port Elizabeth.
15 July 2000	England's Alec Stewart pulled the hat over the face of a streaker during NatWest ODI match between England and the West Indies at the Riverside Ground, Chester-le-Street, Durham.
22 July 2000	A streaker ran on to the pitch and greeted batsman Graham Thorpe during the final of the NatWest Triangular series between England and Zimbabwe at Lord's.
5th August 2000	A streaker jumped the bails on day three of the third Cornhill Test match between England and the West Indies at Old Trafford, Manchester.
20th May 2001	A streaker ran past the players during the fourth day's play in the first npower Test match between England and Pakistan at Lord's.
May 2003	A streaker hurdled the wicket shortly before England's victory over Zimbabwe in the Triangular ODI final at Lord's.

⌒ SUCCESSFUL 4TH-INNINGS RUN CHASES ⌒

Only three countries have successfully chased a fourth-innings target in excess of 400 runs in Test matches. England were involved in one of those games when, looking for a win, they declared 404 ahead of Australia at the start of the final day of the fourth Test at Headingley in 1948. However, the Aussies rattled off the runs in 114 overs for a famous victory that also clinched the series. The top five successful run chases are:

Pos.	Runs	Teams	Venue	Year
1.	418-7	West Indies (v Australia)	St John's	2002/03
2.	406-4	India (v West Indies)	Port of Spain	1975/76
3.	404-3	Australia (v England)	Leeds	1948
4.	369-6	Australia (v Pakistan)	Hobart	1999/2000
5.	362-7	Australia (v West Indies)	Georgetown	1977/78

III

⟶ IAN BOTHAM, OBE ⟵

Ian Terence Botham was born on 24 November 1955 in Heswall, Cheshire. "Beefy", as he was affectionately nicknamed, is one of England's greatest ever cricketers and one of the best all-rounders the world has ever seen.

Botham began his first-class career in 1974 with Somerset and in 1978 he was named as one of *Wisden*'s Cricketers of the Year. In 1986, after more than a decade with Somerset, he left the county as a protest against the sacking of his friends Joel Garner and Viv Richards. From 1987 to 1991 he played for Worcestershire, and then in 1992 he joined County Championship new boys Durham. Midway through the 1993 season he retired after Durham's match against the touring Australians. He also played for Queensland.

He made his England Test debut on 28 July 1977 in the third Test against Australia. In his 15-year, 102-Test career, he scored 5,200 runs at an average of 33.54 (including 14 centuries), took 383 wickets at an average of 28.40 and held 120 catches. He retired from international cricket shortly after the 1992 World Cup.

Botham was a cricketer who played to the very edge – a big-hitting, swashbuckling batsman and fast-medium swing bowler who, on his day, was more than capable of winning a match on his own. The latter was never more evident than during the 1981 Ashes series, when he almost single-handedly won two games for England from a seemingly impossible position. Indeed, such was his dominance throughout the latter part of the series that it came to be known as "Botham's Ashes". The nation now had a young, aggressive, charismatic talisman that they could rely on to defend England's honour on the field of play.

Botham had the occasional run-in with the tabloids. However, this was merely an indication of the uninhibited manner in which Botham played his cricket. For he was a player who would have the crowd on the edge of their seats, holding their breath in anticipation of him either smashing a six over their heads, or bowling a delivery that would scatter the stumps or induce a rash shot.

Away from cricket, Botham championed the cause of leukaemia patients and led long-distance charity walks, such as from Land's End to John O'Groats, raising a great deal of money for many worthy causes. Today Beefy is a respected cricket commentator for Sky TV and can often be seen on television in Shredded Wheat cereal advertisements promoting healthy eating. The enduring memory, however, will be of his inspiring performances against the Australians – and he will always be a hero to England fans.

III

◦ THE GREAT TEST MATCHES (4) ◦

From 17 to 22 December 1954, England played Australia at the Sydney Cricket Ground in the second Test of the 1954–55 Ashes series. The match was a high point for English cricket during a successful decade, whilst Australia were still coming to terms with life without Donald Bradman. In the post-war period up until 1954–55, Bradman and then Lindsay Hassett, who succeeded The Don as captain of Australia, had led their country in eight rubbers and had won all of them except for the two most recent series.

With new skipper Ian Johnson missing, Australia appointed Arthur Morris captain for the Sydney Test. One major change to the England team was the decision to omit Alec Bedser and replace him in the side with off-spinner Bob Appleyard. In the first Test of this Ashes series, played in Brisbane, England had suffered a beating by the Australians by an innings and 154 runs. Much blame for the annihilation was placed on England's unbalanced attack, comprising a battery of pace bowlers with no specialist spinner to add variety. Appleyard and left arm spinner Johnny Wardle rectified that at traditionally spin-friendly Sydney. Godfrey Evans and Tom Graveney were also included, with Reg Simpson, Keith Andrew and Denis Compton, besides Bedser, missing out.

The home side won the toss for this five-day match and decided to put England in. Things did not get off to a good start for the tourists when Trevor Bailey, opening the batting, was out for a duck, bowled by Ray Lindwall. Indeed England were all out for just 154 inside 55 overs, with Wardle the top-scorer on 35. By close of play on day one, Australia had reached 18 for 1, skipper Morris having gone for 12 – caught by Len Hutton off Bailey. The following day Australia added a further 210 runs to be all out for 228, Ron Archer top-scoring with 49 and Frank Tyson and Bailey taking four wickets each.

England began the third day trailing the home side by 74 runs. By the close, England were sitting on 204 for 4, with Peter May just two runs away from his century and Bill Edrich 16 not out. On day four, May duly reached his hundred, but was out for 104 as England reached 296 all out. Australia began their second innings needing 223 to win and at the end of the day's play they were on 72 for 2 (Jim Burke 13 not out and Neil Harvey 26 not out). However, on the fifth day Australia collapsed dramatically and were all out for 184, leaving England with a 38-run victory. Surprisingly it was England fast bowlers, Tyson and Brian Statham, who were the architects of Australia's misfortune, the former taking 6 for 85 to end the match with figures of 10 for 130.

III

AUSTRALIA V ENGLAND – Second Test

17–22 DECEMBER 1954, SYDNEY CRICKET GROUND, AUSTRALIA
Result: England won by 38 runs. *Toss:* Australia. *Umpires:* MJ McInnes, RJJ Wright.

ENGLAND

Batsman	1st innings			2nd innings		
*L Hutton	c Davidson	b Johnston	30	c Benaud	b Johnston	28
TE Bailey		b Lindwall	0	c Langley	b Archer	6
PBH May	c Johnston	b Archer	5		b Lindwall	104
TW Graveney	c Favell	b Johnston	21	c Langley	b Johnston	0
MC Cowdrey	c Langley	b Davidson	23	c Archer	b Benaud	54
WJ Edrich	c Benaud	b Archer	10		b Archer	29
FH Tyson		b Lindwall	0		b Lindwall	9
†TG Evans	c Langley	b Archer	3	c Lindwall	b Archer	4
JH Wardle	c Burke	b Johnston	35	lbw	b Lindwall	8
R Appleyard	c Hole	b Davidson	8	not out		19
JB Statham	not out		14	c Langley	b Johnston	25
Extras	(lb 5)		5	(lb 6, nb 4)		10
TOTAL	(all out)		154	(all out)		296

1/14, 2/19, 3/58, 4/63, 5/84
6/85, 7/88, 8/99, 9/111, 10/154

1/18, 2/55, 3/55, 4/171, 5/222
6/232, 7/239, 8/249, 9/250, 10/296

Bowling: *First Innings:* Lindwall 17–3–47–2, Archer 12–7–12–3, Davidson 12–3–34–2, Johnston 13.3–1–56–3. *Second Innings:* Lindwall 31–10–69–3, Archer 22–9–53–3, Davidson 13–2–52–0, Johnston 19.3–2–70–3, Benaud 19–3–42–1.

AUSTRALIA

Batsman	1st innings			2nd innings		
LE Favell	c Graveney	b Bailey	26	c Edrich	b Tyson	16
*AR Morris	c Hutton	b Bailey	12	lbw	b Statham	10
JW Burke	c Graveney	b Bailey	44		b Tyson	14
RN Harvey	c Cowdrey	b Tyson	12	not out		92
GB Hole		b Tyson	12		b Tyson	0
R Benaud	lbw	b Statham	20	c Tyson	b Appleyard	12
RG Archer	c Hutton	b Tyson	49		b Tyson	6
AK Davidson		b Statham	20	c Evans	b Statham	5
RR Lindwall	c Evans	b Tyson	19		b Tyson	8
†GRA Langley		b Bailey	5		b Statham	0
WA Johnston	not out		0	c Evans	b Tyson	11
Extras	(b 5, lb 2, nb 2)		9	(lb 7, nb 3)		10
TOTAL	(all out)		228	(all out)		184

1/18, 2/65, 3/100, 4/104, 5/122
6/141, 7/193, 8/213, 9/224, 10/228

1/27, 2/34, 3/77, 4/77, 5/102
6/122, 7/127, 8/136, 9/145, 10/184

Bowling: *First Innings:* Statham 18–1–83–2, Bailey 17.4–3–59–4, Tyson 13–2–45–4, Appleyard 7–1–32–0. *Second Innings:* Statham 19–6–45–3, Bailey 6–0–21–0, Tyson 18.4–1–85–6, Appleyard 6–1–12–1, Wardle 4–2–11–0.

II

~ FANTASY ENGLAND XI (5) ~

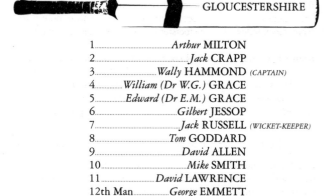

GLOUCESTERSHIRE

1	*Arthur* MILTON
2	*Jack* CRAPP
3	*Wally* HAMMOND *(CAPTAIN)*
4	*William (Dr W.G.)* GRACE
5	*Edward (Dr E.M.)* GRACE
6	*Gilbert* JESSOP
7	*Jack* RUSSELL *(WICKET-KEEPER)*
8	*Tom* GODDARD
9	*David* ALLEN
10	*Mike* SMITH
11	*David* LAWRENCE
12th Man	*George* EMMETT

Did You Know That?
Gloucestershire CCC was officially founded in 1871 although the record books will show that cricket was first played in the county in 1729. The county's greatest ever player was W.G. Grace whose father, Dr H.M. Grace, was involved with its formation. Remarkably, Gloucestershire are one of only four counties that have never won the County Championship.

~ ASHES FEVER (5) ~

"That's up there with my best innings. I've been working hard on my batting – four years ago I was a complete rabbit."
Matthew Hoggard *after his eight not out had helped to win the Fourth Test of the 2005 Ashes*

~ ENGLAND'S MASTER BLASTER ~

During the 1985 Ashes Test against Australia at Edgbaston, Ian Botham walked out to bat with England on 572 for 4. Botham hit the first ball he received from fast bowler Craig McDermott down the ground for a six. It was just one of 80 sixes Beefy hit that summer, which is a record in first-class cricket. The previous best was by Arthur Wellard, another Somerset batsman, who hit 66 sixes in 1935.

II

⟶ COOK'S IN THE BOOK ⟵

Alastair Cook's century and half-century for England in the drawn first
Test against India in Nagpur in March 2006 meant he became only the
fifth English batsman to score a century and half-century on his Test
debut. Cook followed in the footsteps of some very famous names:

Kumar Ranjitsinhji, 62 & 154 not out v Australia, Old Trafford, 1896.
George Gunn, 119 & 74 v Australia, Sydney, 1907.
Paul Gibb, 93 & 106 v South Africa, Johannesburg, 1938.
Andrew Strauss, 112 & 83 v New Zealand, Lord's, 2004.
Alastair Cook, 60 & 104 not out, v India, Nagpur, 2006.

⟶ TOP 5 CAREER BOWLING AVERAGES ⟵

Five English bowlers occupy the top five places in the list of those
who have achieved the best bowling averages during their Test
careers (a minimum of 2,000 balls delivered):

Pos.	Average	Player	Balls	Wkts
1.	10.75 runs per wkt	George Lohmann (ENG)	3,830	112
2.	12.70 runs per wkt	John Ferris (ENG/AUS)	2,302	61
3.	15.54 runs per wkt	Billy Barnes (ENG)	2,289	51
4.	16.42 runs per wkt	Billy Bates (ENG)	2,364	50
5.	16.43 runs per wkt	Sydney Barnes (ENG)	7,873	189

Excluding the 2,000 balls rule, the best career average is actually
0.00 runs per wicket. Albert "Monkey" Hornby (England) took 1
wicket without conceding a run in the 28 balls he bowled; Wilf
Barber (England) took 1 wicket without conceding a run in the 2
balls he bowled; and Bruce Murray (New Zealand) took 1 wicket
without conceding a run from 6 balls.

⟶ HIGHEST TEST AVERAGE FOR AN OPENER ⟵

Herbert Sutcliffe, of Yorkshire and England, holds the record for
the highest Test batting average for an opener with 60.73. Sutcliffe
opened 83 times for England in Tests, scoring 64 on his debut
against South Africa at Edgbaston in 1924. Sutcliffe's overall average
never dipped below 60 during his entire 54-Test career.[†]

*[†]Herbert Sutcliffe was also the first batsman to score a hundred in each innings of a Test on two
occasions – in 1925 and 1929.*

Ⅲ

~ *WISDEN* CRICKETERS OF THE YEAR ~

1889 J Briggs, JJ Ferris, GA Lohmann, R Peel, CTB Turner,
SMJ Woods

1890 R Abel, W Barnes, W Gunn, L Hall, R Henderson,
JM Read, A Shrewsbury, FH Sugg, A Ward

1891 JM Blackham, G MacGregor, R Pilling, M Sherwin,
H Wood

1892 W Attewell, JT Hearne, F Martin, AW Mold, JW Sharpe

1893 HT Hewett, LCH Palairet, WW Read, SW Scott,
AE Stoddart

1894 G Giffen, A Hearne, FS Jackson, GHS Trott, E Wainwright

1895 W Brockwell, JT Brown, CB Fry, TW Hayward, AC MacLaren

1896 WG Grace

1897 SE Gregory, AFA Lilley, KS Ranjitsinhji, T Richardson,
H Trumble

1898 FG Bull, WR Cuttell, NF Druce, GL Jessop, JR Mason

1899 WH Lockwood, W Rhodes, W Storer, CL Townsend,
AE Trott

1900 J Darling, C Hill, AO Jones, MA Noble, RM Poore

1901 RE Foster, S Haigh, GH Hirst, TL Taylor, J Tunnicliffe

1902 LC Braund, CP McGahey, F Mitchell, WG Quaife,
JT Tyldesley

1903 WW Armstrong, CJ Burnup, J Iremonger, JJ Kelly,
VT Trumper

1904 C Blythe, JR Gunn, AE Knight, W Mead, PF Warner

1905 BJT Bosanquet, EA Halliwell, J Hallows, PA Perrin,
RH Spooner

1906 D Denton, WS Lees, GJ Thompson, J Vine, LG Wright

1907 JN Crawford, A Fielder, EG Hayes, KL Hutchings, NA Knox

1908 AW Hallam, RO Schwarz, FA Tarrant, AEE Vogler, TG Wass

1909 W Brearley, Lord Hawke, JB Hobbs, A Marshal, JT Newstead

1910 W Bardsley, SF Barnes, DW Carr, AP Day, VS Ransford

1911 HK Foster, A Hartley, CB Llewellyn, WC Smith, FE Woolley

1912 FR Foster, JW Hearne, SP Kinneir, CP Mead, H Strudwick

1913 J Wisden

1914 MW Booth, G Gunn, JW Hitch, AE Relf, Lord Tennyson

1915 JWHT Douglas, PGH Fender, HTW Hardinge, DJ Knight,
SG Smith

1918 HL Calder, JDE Firth, CH Gibson, GA Rotherham,
GTS Stevens

1919 PW Adams, APF Chapman, AC Gore, LP Hedges,
NE Partridge

1920 A Ducat, EH Hendren, P Holmes, H Sutcliffe, GE Tyldesley
1921 PF Warner
1922 H Ashton, JL Bryan, JM Gregory, CG Macartney,
EA McDonald
1923 AW Carr, AP Freeman, CWL Parker, CAG Russell,
A Sandham
1924 AER Gilligan, R Kilner, GG Macaulay, CH Parkin,
MW Tate
1925 RH Catterall, JCW MacBryan, HW Taylor, RK Tyldesley,
WW Whysall
1926 JB Hobbs
1927 G Geary, H Larwood, J Mercer, WAS Oldfield, WM Woodfull
1928 RC Blunt, C Hallows, WR Hammond, DR Jardine,
VWC Jupp
1929 LEG Ames, G Duckworth, M Leyland, SJ Staples, JC White
1930 EH Bowley, KS Duleepsinhji, HGO Owen-Smith,
RWV Robins, RES Wyatt
1931 DG Bradman, CV Grimmett, BH Lyon, IAR Peebles,
MJL Turnbull
1932 WE Bowes, CS Dempster, J Langridge, Nawab of Pataudi,
H Verity
1933 WE Astill, FR Brown, AS Kennedy, CK Nayudu, W Voce
1934 AH Bakewell, GA Headley, MS Nichols, LF Townsend,
CF Walters
1935 SJ McCabe, WJ O'Reilly, GAE Paine, WH Ponsford,
CIJ Smith
1936 HB Cameron, ERT Holmes, B Mitchell, D Smith,
AW Wellard
1937 CJ Barnett, WH Copson, AR Gover, VM Merchant,
TS Worthington
1938 TWJ Goddard, J Hardstaff, L Hutton, JH Parks, E Paynter
1939 HT Bartlett, WA Brown, DCS Compton, K Farnes, A Wood
1940 LN Constantine, WJ Edrich, WW Keeton, WFF Price,
AB Sellers
1947 AV Bedser, LB Fishlock, MH Mankad, TPB Smith,
C Washbrook
1948 MP Donnelly, A Melville, AD Nourse, JDB Robertson,
NWD Yardley
1949 AL Hassett, WA Johnston, RR Lindwall, AR Morris,
D Tallon
1950 TE Bailey, RO Jenkins, JG Langridge, RT Simpson, B
Sutcliffe

Ⅲ

1951 TG Evans, S Ramadhin, AL Valentine, ED Weekes,
FMM Worrell

1952 R Appleyard, HE Dollery, JC Laker, PBH May, EAB Rowan

1953 H Gimblett, TW Graveney, DS Sheppard, WS Surridge,
FS Trueman

1954 RN Harvey, GAR Lock, KR Miller, JH Wardle, W Watson

1955 B Dooland, Fazal Mahmood, WE Hollies, JB Statham,
GE Tribe

1956 MC Cowdrey, DJ Insole, DJ McGlew, HJ Tayfield, FH Tyson

1957 D Brookes, JW Burke, MJ Hilton, GRA Langley,
PE Richardson

1958 PJ Loader, AJW McIntyre, OG Smith, MJ Stewart, CL Walcott

1959 HL Jackson, RE Marshall, CA Milton, JR Reid, D Shackleton

1960 KF Barrington, DB Carr, R Illingworth, G Pullar, MJK Smith

1961 NAT Adcock, ER Dexter, RA McLean, R Subba Row,
JV Wilson

1962 WE Alley, R Benaud, AK Davidson, WM Lawry, NC O'Neill

1963 D Kenyon, Mushtaq Mohammad, PH Parfitt, PJ Sharpe,
FJ Titmus

1964 DB Close, CC Griffith, CC Hunte, RB Kanhai, GS Sobers

1965 G Boycott, PJP Burge, JA Flavell, GD McKenzie, RB Simpson

1966 KC Bland, JH Edrich, RC Motz, PM Pollock, RG Pollock

1967 RW Barber, BL D'Oliveira, C Milburn, JT Murray, SM Nurse

1968 Asif Iqbal, Hanif Mohammad, K Higgs, JM Parks,
MAK Pataudi

1969 JG Binks, DM Green, BA Richards, DL Underwood,
OS Wheatley

1970 BF Butcher, APE Knott, Majid Khan, MJ Procter, DJ Shepherd

1971 JD Bond, CH Lloyd, BW Luckhurst, GM Turner, RT Virgin

1972 GG Arnold, BS Chandrasekhar, LR Gibbs, B Taylor,
Zaheer Abbas

1973 GS Chappell, DK Lillee, RAL Massie, JA Snow, KR Stackpole

1974 KD Boyce, BE Congdon, KWR Fletcher, RC Fredericks,
PJ Sainsbury

1975 DL Amiss, MH Denness, N Gifford, AW Greig, AME Roberts

1976 IM Chappell, PG Lee, RB McCosker, DS Steele, RA Woolmer

1977 JM Brearley, CG Greenidge, MA Holding, IVA Richards,
RW Taylor

1978 IT Botham, M Hendrick, A Jones, KS McEwan, RGD Willis

1979 DI Gower, JK Lever, CM Old, CT Radley, JN Shepherd

1980 J Garner, SM Gavaskar, GA Gooch, DW Randall, BC Rose

1981 KJ Hughes, RD Jackman, AJ Lamb, CEB Rice,
VAP van der Bijl

III

1982 TM Alderman, AR Border, RJ Hadlee, Javed Miandad, RW Marsh

1983 Imran Khan, TE Jesty, AI Kallicharran, Kapil Dev, MD Marshall

1984 M Amarnath, JV Coney, JE Emburey, MW Gatting, CL Smith

1985 MD Crowe, HA Gomes, GW Humpage, J Simmons, S Wettimuny

1986 P Bainbridge, RM Ellison, CJ McDermott, NV Radford, RT Robinson

1987 JH Childs, GA Hick, DB Vengsarkar, CA Walsh, JJ Whitaker

1988 JP Agnew, NA Foster, DP Hughes, PM Roebuck, Saleem Malik

1989 KJ Barnett, PJL Dujon, PA Neale, FD Stephenson, SR Waugh

1990 SJ Cook, DM Jones, RC Russell, RA Smith, MA Taylor

1991 MA Atherton, M Azharuddin, AR Butcher, DL Haynes, ME Waugh

1992 CEL Ambrose, PAJ DeFreitas, AA Donald, RB Richardson, Waqar Younis

1993 NE Briers, MD Moxon, IDK Salisbury, AJ Stewart, Wasim Akram

1994 DC Boon, IA Healy, MG Hughes, SK Warne, SL Watkin

1995 BC Lara, DE Malcolm, TA Munton, SJ Rhodes, KC Wessels

1996 DG Cork, PA de Silva, ARC Fraser, A Kumble, DA Reeve

1997 ST Jayasuriya, Mushtaq Ahmed, Saeed Anwar, PV Simmons, SR Tendulkar

1998 MTG Elliott, SG Law, GD McGrath, MP Maynard, GP Thorpe

1999 ID Austin, D Gough, M Muralitharan, A Ranatunga, JN Rhodes

2000 CL Cairns, RS Dravid, L Klusener, TM Moody, Saqlain Mushtaq

2001 MW Alleyne, MP Bicknell, AR Caddick, JL Langer, DS Lehmann

2002 A Flower, AC Gilchrist, JN Gillespie, VVS Laxman, DR Martyn

2003 ML Hayden, AJ Hollioake, N Hussain, SM Pollock, MP Vaughan

2004 CJ Adams, A Flintoff, IJ Harvey, G Kirsten, GC Smith

2005 AF Giles, SJ Harmison, RWT Key, AJ Strauss, ME Trescothick

2006 MJ Hoggard, SP Jones, B Lee, KP Pietersen, RT Ponting

Did You Know That?

The Wisden Almanack was established in England in 1864.

Ⅲ

Surrey's Peter May led England in the 1956 home Ashes series. He is widely considered to have been the finest English batsman of the post-war era, a player who had the full array of classical shots in his locker. In 1954/55, May was Len Hutton's vice-captain for England's tour of Australia and when Hutton was struck down with lumbago prior to the 1955 series against South Africa, May took over as captain. When May made his Test debut in 1951 he became an integral part of two of the most successful sides English cricket has ever seen. From 1952 to 1958 Surrey won seven consecutive County Championships, with May leading the side to glory in 1957 and 1958, whilst England did not lose a Test series during the same period.

Going into the fourth Test at Old Trafford, Manchester, the 1956 Ashes series was all-square at 1–1 following England's victory in the previous match at Headingley. At Old Trafford, England won the toss and May elected to bat. Peter Richardson and Colin Cowdrey opened for England and between them they racked up 184, with Richardson scoring a century (104). At the end of the first day, England were placed nicely on 307 for 3 (Reverend David Sheppard 59 not out and Trevor Bailey 14 not out), after May had been caught by Ron Archer off the bowling of Richie Benaud for 43. When play resumed on the second day, Sheppard went on to reach his hundred (113) as Australia bowled England all out for 459.

It was at this point that matters took a truly amazing turn, literally. On a rain-affected pitch, England proceeded to bowl Australia out for 84 with Jim Laker, the Surrey off-spinner, taking 9 for 37, including the last 7 Australian wickets for a mere 8 runs in 22 balls. Laker had previously taken 11 wickets for 113 to help England beat Australia by an innings and 42 runs at Headingley. A shell-shocked Australia were forced to follow on 375 runs behind. Yet after taking nine wickets in the first innings, Laker went one better in the second, taking all 10 wickets for just 53 runs in 51.2 overs as Australia were bowled out for 205. England won by an innings and 170 runs and, not surprisingly, it became known as Laker's Test. His figures of 19 for 90 have never been bettered in Test cricket and likely never will be. The other wicket-taker for England was Laker's Surrey spin colleague Tony Lock, who finished with match figures of 1 for 106 from his 69 overs.

Did You Know That?
Besides being a Test record, Jim Laker's 19 wickets in the match is a record for first-class cricket and his 46 wickets in the series (at 9.60) is also a record for England versus Australia

ENGLAND V AUSTRALIA – Fourth Test

26–31 JULY 1956, OLD TRAFFORD, MANCHESTER

Result: England won by an innings and 170 runs. *Toss:* England. *Umpires:* DE Davies, FS Lee.

ENGLAND

PE Richardson	c Maddocks	b Benaud	104
MC Cowdrey	c Maddocks	b Lindwall	80
DS Sheppard		b Archer	113
*PBH May	c Archer	b Benaud	43
TE Bailey		b Johnson	20
C Washbrook	lbw	b Johnson	6
ASM Oakman	c Archer	b Johnson	10
†TG Evans	st Maddocks	b Johnson	47
JC Laker	run out		3
GAR Lock	not out		25
JB Statham	c Maddocks	b Lindwall	0
Extras	(b 2, lb 5, w 1)		8
TOTAL	(all out)		459

1/153, 2/195, 3/288, 4/321. 5/327
6/339, 7/401, 8/417, 9/458, 10/459

Bowling: *First Innings:* Lindwall 21.3–6–63–2, Miller 21–6–41–0, Archer 22–6–73–1, Johnson 47–10–151–4, Benaud 47–17–123–2.

AUSTRALIA

CC McDonald	c Lock	b Laker	32		c Oakman	b Laker	89
JW Burke	c Cowdrey	b Lock	22		c Lock	b Laker	33
RN Harvey		b Laker	0		c Cowdrey	b Laker	0
ID Craig	lbw	b Laker	8		lbw	b Laker	38
KR Miller	c Oakman	b Laker	6		(6)	b Laker	0
KD Mackay	c Oakman	b Laker	0		(5) c Oakman	b Laker	0
RG Archer	st Evans	b Laker	6		c Oakman	b Laker	0
R Benaud	c Statham	b Laker	0			b Laker	18
RR Lindwall	not out		6		c Lock	b Laker	8
†LV Maddocks		b Laker	4		(11) lbw	b Laker	2
*IWG Johnson		b Laker	0		(10) not out		1
Extras			0		(b 12, lb 4)		16
TOTAL	(all out)		84		(all out)		205

1/48, 2/48, 3/62, 4/62, 5/62   *1/28, 2/55, 3/114, 4/124, 5/130*
6/73, 7/73, 8/78, 9/84, 10/84   *6/130, 7/181, 8/198, 9/203, 10/205*

Bowling: *First Innings:* Statham 6–3–6–0, Bailey 4–3–4—0, Laker 16.4–4–37–9, Lock 14–3–37–1.
Second Innings: Statham 16–10–15–0, Bailey 20–8–31–0, Laker 51.2–23–53–10, Lock 55–30–69–0, Oakman 8–3–21–0.

⚏

⇝ BEEFY AND LAMBY TOPS ON TV ⇜

In March 2006, a series of television advertisements featuring former England stars Ian Botham and Allan Lamb appeared on British television promoting English beef and lamb. Put on the back foot by Mad Cow Disease and the Foot and Mouth panic, red meat lovers are no longer batting on a sticky wicket.

⇝ ASHES FEVER (6) ⇜

"No one thought the 1981 Botham Ashes series could ever be repeated, but this exceeded it. The excitement and nail-biting action has been unbelievable."
Bob Willis *reflects on the 2005 Ashes*

⇝ MOST RUNS SCORED IN A SERIES ⇜

England's Wally Hammond comes second in the list of those who have scored the most runs in a Test series:

Pos. Runs	Player	Series & Year
1. 974 runs (7 innings)	Don Bradman (AUS)	England v Australia, 1930
2. 905 runs (9 innings)	Wally Hammond (ENG)	Australia v England, 1928/29
3. 839 runs (11 innings)	Mark Taylor (AUS)	England v Australia, 1989
4. 834 runs (9 innings)	Neil Harvey (AUS)	Australia v South Africa, 1952/53
5. 829 runs (7 innings)	Viv Richards (WI)	England v West Indies, 1976

⇝ CRAPP PLAYER ⇜

John "Jack" Crapp of Gloucestershire played in seven Test matches for England from 1964 to 1965. There is a story that on one occasion when Crapp was on a tour of South Africa with England he was sharing a room with one of the famous Bedser twins. One night it is believed that Crapp returned to the hotel and as he approached the reception desk, after downing several drinks, the receptionist said: "Bed, sir?". Jack reportedly replied: "No, Crapp", at which point the receptionist discreetly pointed him in the direction of the gentleman's toilets.

♔ FANTASY ENGLAND XI (6) ♔

HAMPSHIRE

1 .... *Edward* WYNYARD
2 .... *Chris* SMITH
3 .... *Paul* TERRY
4 .... *Phil (C.P.)* MEAD
5 .... *Robin* SMITH *(CAPTAIN)*
6 .... *Kevin* PIETERSEN
7 .... *Lionel (Lord)* TENNYSON *(WICKET-KEEPER)*
8 .... *Derek* SHACKLETON
9 .... *Butch* WHITE
10 .... *Shaun* UDAL
11 .... *Bob* COTTAM
12th Man .... *George* BROWN

Did You Know That?
Hampshire CCC first played first-class cricket in 1864, and in 1895, took part in the County Championship for the first time. The County has won the County Championship twice (1961 and 1973).

♔ FIRST AND LAST IN EQUAL MEASURE ♔

Legendary Australian cricketer Greg Chappell scored a century in his first Test innings, hitting 108 against England in Perth in 1970/71, and in his last Test innings, in Sydney in 1983/84, when he made 182 against Pakistan. India's Mohammad Azharuddin is the only other Test cricketer to have achieved this feat. He scored 110 in his first Test, against England in Calcutta in 1984/85, and in his 99th and last ever Test match, against South Africa in Bangalore in 1999/2000, he hit 102.

♔ LARA TAMES ENGLISH LIONS ♔

On Sunday 11 April 2004, day three of the fourth and final Test match between England and the West Indies at the Recreation Ground in St John's, Antigua, Brian Lara reached a Test record 400 not out. The entire crowd leapt to their feet and greeted Lara with ecstatic applause in acknowledgement of this magnificent and historic achievement.

III

⁓ THE BLACK PRINCE OF CRICKETERS ⁓

Kumar Shri Ranjitsinhji was born on 10 September 1872 in Sarodar, a small village in the western Indian province of Kathiawar. "Ranji" – as he was affectionately known – played for Cambridge University, Sussex and England. Amazingly, he had never played an organized game of cricket before he arrived at Cambridge in 1891 and yet won a Blue in his final year. A brilliant improviser with the bat, he invented the leg glance and is widely regarded as one of the greatest batsmen the game has ever seen. He was nicknamed the "Black Prince of Cricketers", and Neville Cardus once described him as "the Midsummer night's dream of cricket". He played his first county match at Lord's in May 1895, and in 1896 he became the first Indian to play Test cricket when he made his debut for England.

He scored 62 and 154 not out at Old Trafford against Australia, becoming only the second batsman after W.G. Grace to score a century on his debut for England and also the first Test batsman to score a century before lunch. In 1897 he scored 175 in the first innings of his first overseas Test, also against Australia, which at the time was the highest score that had been made for England in Test cricket. Ranji played in 15 Test matches for England from 1896 to 1902, scoring 989 runs at an average of 44.95. In 1897, the year of Queen Victoria's Jubilee, he was named a *Wisden* Cricketer of the Year. Away from cricket, Ranji was appointed the Maharaja Jam Sahib of Nawanagar in 1907, was Chancellor of the Indian Chamber of Princes, and represented India at the League of Nations. His official title was Colonel H. H. Shri Sir Ranjitsinhji Vibhaji, Jam Sahib of Nawanagar GBE KCSI. Ranji died on 2nd April 1933. The Ranji Trophy, India's premier first-class cricket tournament, was named in his honour and inaugurated in 1935 by the Maharaja Bhupindra Singh of Patiala.

⁓ TOP FIVE TEST STUMPERS ⁓

England's Godfrey Evans lies in second place in the table for the highest number of Test stumpings in a career:

Pos.	Stumpings	Player
1.	52	Bert Oldfield (AUS)
2.	46	Godfrey Evans (ENG)
3.	38	Syed Kirmani (IND)
4.	35	Adam Gilchrist (AUS)
5.	29	Ian Healy (AUS)

Ⅲ

⟶ GEOFFREY BOYCOTT, OBE ⟵

Geoffrey Boycott was born on 21 October 1940 in Fitzwilliam, Yorkshire, and began playing county cricket for Yorkshire in 1962. He made his Test debut in the 1964 Ashes series against Australia. In the first Test at Trent Bridge he opened alongside Fred Titmus, scoring 48. He was named as one of the *Wisden* Cricketers of the Year the following year.

In both County Championship and Test cricket Boycott gained a reputation for being sparing with the attacking strokes. Nevertheless, he went on to score 8,114 runs in an 18-year Test career spanning 108 Test matches. He was the first England cricketer to exceed 8,000 Test runs and is still in fourth place on England's all-time run-scoring list (only Graham Gooch, Alec Stewart and David Gower are above him). Boycott averaged 47.73 runs over 193 innings whilst an indication of how valuable his batting was to England is reflected by the fact that only 20 of his Tests ended in defeat.

When England needed a new captain in 1974, many cricket commentators thought that Boycott, rather than Mike Denness, should have succeeded Ray Illingworth. Always a controversial figure, Boycott then spent three years (1974–77) in self-imposed exile from the England team. He claimed he had simply lost his appetite for Test cricket, although many believed it was because the England selectors did not pick him as the captain of the England.

However, there is little doubt that had he not taken a three-year sabbatical he would have made 10,000 Test runs. In 1977, Boycott made a triumphant return to the England side in the third Test against Australia at Trent Bridge, batting on each of the first three days on his way to 107 in England's first innings. He then scored 80 not out in the second innings, which spanned the fourth and fifth days. In the next Test, in front of his adoring home fans at Headingley, "Sir Geoffrey" became the first ever cricketer to score his hundredth first-class century in a Test match, when he scored 191. His Test career included 22 centuries (an England record that he holds jointly with Wally Hammond and Colin Cowdrey).

Boycott was appointed vice-captain of England for the 1977/78 tour of Pakistan and New Zealand, and when Mike Brearley was injured during the tour, he was made captain. His highest ever Test score was 246 not out which he scored in 1967. Not really an all-rounder, Boycott was a useful medium-pace change bowler and he took seven Test wickets at an average of 54.57. After he retired he became a well-respected cricket commentator.

▥
⌐ THE WETHERALL AWARD ⌐

The Wetherall Award is given by the Cricket Society to the leading all-rounder in English first-class cricket:

1967	Fred Titmus (*Middlesex*)
1968	John Shepherd (*Kent*)
1969	Mushtaq Mohammad (*Northamptonshire*)
1970	Garfield Sobers (*Nottinghamshire*)
1971	Peter Sainsbury (*Hampshire*)
1972	Keith Boyce (*Essex*)
1973	Robin Jackman (*Surrey*)
1974	Stuart Turner (*Essex*)
1975	Ray Illingworth (*Leicestershire*)
1976	Imran Khan (*Worcestershire*)
1977	Clive Rice (*Nottinghamshire*)
1978	Mike Procter (*Gloucestershire*)
1979	Clive Rice (*Nottinghamshire*)
1980	Imran Khan (*Sussex*)
1981	Clive Rice (*Nottinghamshire*)
1982	Richard Hadlee (*Nottinghamshire*)
1983	Paddy Clift (*Leicestershire*)
1984	Richard Hadlee (*Nottinghamshire*)
1985	Rodney Ontong (*Glamorgan*)
1986	Richard Hadlee (*Nottinghamshire & New Zealand*)
1987	Richard Hadlee (*Nottinghamshire*)
1988	Franklyn Stephenson (*Nottinghamshire*)
1989	David Capel (*Northamptonshire*)
1990	Malcolm Marshall (*Hampshire*)
1992	Chris Lewis (*Nottinghamshire*)
1993	John Emburey (*Middlesex*)
1994	Franklyn Stephenson (*Sussex*)
1995	Chris Cairns (*Nottinghamshire*)
1996	Phil Simmons (*Leicestershire*)
1997	Graham Rose (*Somerset*)
1998	Gavin Hamilton (*Yorkshire*)
1999	Ronnie Irani (*Essex*)
2000	Martin Bicknell (*Surrey*)
2001	Martin Bicknell (*Surrey*)
2002	Darren Maddy (*Leicestershire*)
2003	Mike Kasprowicz (*Glamorgan*)
2004	Robert Croft (*Glamorgan*)
2005	Shane Warne (*Hampshire & Australia*)

III

⤳ ENGLAND'S TEST MATCH GROUNDS ⤳

Official name (known as)	City	Date first used
The BRIT Oval Cricket Ground (The Oval)	London	6th September 1880
Old Trafford Cricket Ground (Old Trafford)	Manchester	10th July 1884
Lord's Cricket Ground (Lord's)	London	21st July 1884
Trent Bridge Ground (Trent Bridge)	Nottingham	1st June 1899
County Cricket Ground (Headingley)	Leeds	29th June 1899
County Cricket Ground (Edgbaston)	Birmingham	29th May 1902
Bramall Lane*	Sheffield	3rd July 1902
County Ground (Riverside)	Chester-le-Street	5th June 2003

* Staged only one Test, and the ground has not been used for cricket since 1973

⤳ REBEL TOURS TO SOUTH AFRICA ⤳

During the 1970s and 1980s, South Africa was banned from world cricket as a direct result of the apartheid regime that was prevalent in the country at the time. However, during the 1980s, South Africa induced a number of the world's best cricketers to play in tour matches in the country. The games were given Test status in South Africa but not by the cricket world's governing body. The following England players captained a Rebel Tour side:

Name	Year	P	W	L	D
Graham Gooch	1981/82	3	0	1	2
Mike Gatting	1989/90	1	0	1	0

⤳ HOOKED ON TONY ⤳

Tony Greig captained England in the Centenary Test at the MCG in March 1977. During Australia's second innings, debutant batsman David Hookes struck Greig's off-spin for five consecutive boundaries in one over. Greig lost the England captaincy in 1977 when he teamed up with Kerry Packer's World Series Cricket. One year later, Greig left his county club, Sussex, after being offered a "job for life" by Packer.

The third Wisden Trophy series took place in 1967/68 in the West Indies, with the home side favourites to win the trophy for the third consecutive time. However, the two sides entered the fourth Test at Port of Spain, Trinidad, all square after three draws. The West Indies, captained by the legendary Garfield Sobers, won the toss, chose to bat, and at the end of a rain-affected first day's play were nicely placed on 168 for 2. By close of play on the second day, the home side had racked up an impressive 479 for 4, with both Seymour Nurse (136) and Rohan Kanhai (153) having recorded centuries. Sobers declared on day three, the West Indies having reached 526 for 7, despite stoppages, at a rate of four per over.

England, led by Colin Cowdrey, replied with 404 all out to trail the home side by 122 runs, the skipper himself top-scoring with 148 and Geoffrey Boycott and wicket-keeper Alan Knott chiming in with sixties. There then followed one of the most notable episodes in Test cricket history. At 92 for 2, Sobers declared the West Indies second innings closed, setting England 215 to win in 165 minutes of play. Sobers' positive declaration set up an exciting finish, England reaching their target with just three minutes of play remaining to win by 7 wickets. In the fifth and final Test, chasing 308 for victory, England managed to hold out for a draw, finishing on 206 for 9 to claim the Wisden Trophy for the first time with a 1–0 series win. Two men stood out above all others in the 1967/68 Wisden Trophy series: Sobers was outstanding with the bat, averaging 90.83, whilst John Snow took 27 wickets in his four Tests, although just 1 for 97 in Port of Spain, at the time the best series haul by an England bowler in the Caribbean.

Season	Host	Tests	England	W Indies	Draw	Winners
1963	England	5	1	3	1	W Indies
1967/68	W Indies	5	1	0	4	England
1969	England	3	2	0	1	England
1984	England	5	0	5	0	W Indies
First W Indies "blackwash"						
1985/86	W Indies	5	0	5	0	W Indies
Second W Indies "blackwash"						
2000	England	5	3	1	1	England
First England victory for 31 years						
2003/04	W Indies	4	3	0	1	England
2004	England	4	4	0	0	England
England's first "whitewash"						

WEST INDIES V ENGLAND – Fourth Test

14–19 MARCH 1968, QUEENS PARK OVAL, PORT OF SPAIN, TRINIDAD

Result: England won by 7 wickets. *Toss:* West Indies. *Umpires:* RG Gosein, D Sang Hue.

WEST INDIES

GS Camacho	c Knott	b Brown	87	c Graveney	b Snow	31
MC Carew	c Lock	b Brown	36	not out		40
SM Nurse	c Edrich	b Barrington	136	run out		9
RB Kanhai	c Barrington	b Lock	153	not out		2
CH Lloyd		b Jones	43			
*GS Sobers	c Jones	b Brown	48			
BF Butcher	not out		7			
WV Rodriguez		b Jones	0			
†DL Murray	not out		5			
CC Griffith						
LR Gibbs						
Extras	(lb 6, nb 5)		11	(b 1, lb 7, nb 2)		10
TOTAL	(for 7 wickets declared)		526	(for 2 wickets declared)		92

1/119, 2/142, 3/415, 4/421, 5/506, 6/513, 7/514   *1/66, 2/88*

Bowling: *First Innings:* Brown 27–2–107–3, Snow 20–3–68–0, Jones 29–1–108–2, D'Oliveira 15–2–62–0, Lock 32–3–129–1, Barrington 10–2–41–1. *Second Innings:* Brown 10–2–33–0, Snow 9–0–29–1, Jones 11–2–20–0.

ENGLAND

JH Edrich	c Lloyd	b Carew	32		b Rodriguez	29
G Boycott	c Nurse	b Rodriguez	62	not out		80
*MC Cowdrey	c Murray	b Butcher	48	c Sobers	b Gibbs	71
KF Barrington	lbw	b Gibbs	48			
TW Graveney	c Murray	b Rodriguez	8	(4)	b Gibbs	2
BL D'Oliveira		b Rodriguez	0	(5) not out		12
†APE Knott	not out		89			
JA Snow		b Butcher	0			
DJ Brown	c Murray	b Butcher	0			
GAR Lock	lbw	b Butcher	3			
IJ Jones		b Butcher	1			
Extras	(b 13, lb 11, w 2, nb 7)		33	(b 11, lb 6, nb 4)		21
TOTAL	(all out)		404	(for 3 wickets)		215

1/86, 2/112, 3/245, 4/260, 5/260   *1/55, 2/173, 3/182*
6/373, 7/377, 8/377, 9/381, 10/404

Bowling: *First Innings:* Sobers 36–8–87–0, Griffith 3–1–7–0, Gibbs 57–24–68–1, Rodriguez 35–4–145–3, Carew 25–18–23–1, Butcher 13.4–2–34–5, Lloyd 4–2–7–0, Nurse 2–2–0–0. *Second Innings:* Sobers 14–0–48–0, Gibbs 16.4–1–76–2, Rodriguez 10–1–34–1, Carew 7–2–19–0, Butcher 5–1–17–0.

III

◦ FANTASY ENGLAND XI (7) ◦

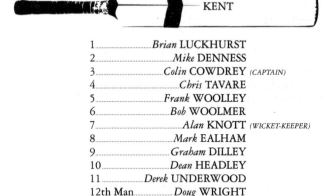

KENT

1	*Brian* LUCKHURST
2	*Mike* DENNESS
3	*Colin* COWDREY *(CAPTAIN)*
4	*Chris* TAVARE
5	*Frank* WOOLLEY
6	*Bob* WOOLMER
7	*Alan* KNOTT *(WICKET-KEEPER)*
8	*Mark* EALHAM
9	*Graham* DILLEY
10	*Dean* HEADLEY
11	*Derek* UNDERWOOD
12th Man	*Doug* WRIGHT

Did You Know That?

The first recorded inter-county match took place in 1709 between Kent and Surrey. Kent CCC has won the County Championship six times (1906, 1909, 1910, 1913, 1970 and 1978) and in 1977 the County shared the Championship with Middlesex.

◦ DUAL CAPTAIN OF ENGLAND ◦

Reginald Erskine "Tip" Foster is the only man to captain England at cricket and football.[†] As a footballer he made his international debut on 28 March 1900 in a 1–1 draw with Wales in Cardiff. In his second game for England he scored twice in a 3–0 win over Ireland on 9 March 1901; he also scored against Wales and Scotland before captaining England in his fifth and last game for his country, a 0–0 draw with Wales. In December 1903 he marked his Test debut with an amazing innings that remains to this day the highest score by a player in his first Test as well as the highest score by an English player on Australian soil. Foster scored 287 as England posted a match-winning total of 577 at Sydney. He played in eight Tests for England, captaining the side against South Africa in 1907. Foster suffered from diabetes and sadly died in 1914, aged just 36.

[†] *R.E. Foster was one of seven Foster brothers who played cricket for Worcestershire in the years before the outbreak of World War 1.*

▮

⌐ ASHES FEVER (7) ⌐

"It's an unbelievable feeling to win the Ashes and it hasn't really sunk in quite what we have achieved yet."
Michael Vaughan, *September 2005*

⌐ KEEDIE'S JERUSALEM ⌐

After the Ashes triumph in the summer of 2005, England's cricketing heroes teamed up with pop songstress Keedie for a jolly rendition of William Blake's classic poem "Jerusalem".

> *And did those feet in ancient time*
> *Walk upon England's mountains green?*
> *And was the holy Lamb of God*
> *On England's pleasant pastures seen?*
>
> *And did the Countenance Divine*
> *Shine forth upon our clouded hills?*
> *And was Jerusalem builded here*
> *Among these dark Satanic mills?*
>
> *Bring me my bow of burning gold:*
> *Bring me my arrows of desire:*
> *Bring me my spear: O clouds, unfold!*
> *Bring me my chariot of fire:*
>
> *I will not cease from mental fight,*
> *Nor shall my sword sleep in my hand,*
> *Till we have built Jerusalem,*
> *In England's green and pleasant land.*

⌐ HIGHEST ODI TOTALS ⌐

England lies fifth in the table of the highest team ODI totals:

Pos.	Score	Overs	Teams	Venue	Year
1.	438–9	49.5	S Africa v Australia	Johannesburg	2005/06
2.	434–4	50	Australia v S Africa	Johannesburg	2005/06
3.	398–5	50	Sri Lanka v Kenya	Kandy	1995/96
4.	397–5	44	New Zealand v Zimbabwe	Bulawayo	2005/06
5.	391–4	50	England v Bangladesh	Nottingham	2005

Ⅲ

⚬ THE BARMY ARMY ⚬

It was the *Sydney Morning Herald* newspaper which originally coined the phrase "Barmy Army" as a grudging term of respect for the hordes of touring England supporters who, despite staring defeat in the face during the disastrous 1994/95 Ashes Test series, never let up throughout the tour with their unwavering and vociferous support for the England players. Today, when England play, it is seldom long before a fan in the crowd, his face usually painted with the flag of St George, starts singing "Everywhere we go-o", whereupon the entire gathering of England's supporters, throughout the ground, join in as one voice. The song ends with a rousing chorus of "Michael Vaughan's Barmy Army, Michael Vaughan's Barmy Army, Michael Vaughan's Barmy Army". Indeed, it has become something of a tradition to see the Pink Panther and Sylvester the Cat supporting England in all of the world's famous cricket grounds.

One of the most appealing features of the Barmy Army is that anyone can become a member, regardless of their age or gender. There are no membership fees to pay: all you are asked to do is simply turn up to a match and join in the fun. The Barmy Army's mission statement, found on their website, is to "make watching cricket more fun and much more popular".

⚬ BOTHAM GIVES FOOTBALL THE BOOT ⚬

Ian Botham was also a talented footballer and had the choice of playing professional football or cricket. Fortunately for English cricket fans he chose to be a cricketer, although later on he did play football for Scunthorpe United in order to get fit after an injury.

⚬ SUPERSUB ⚬

Hanumant Singh of India fielded as a substitute for both India and England in the second Test of the 1961/62 series, held at Green Park, Kanpur. He went on to score a century on his Test debut against England at New Delhi in 1964.

⚬ A LUCKY ESCAPE ⚬

At Sydney in 1932, England opening batsman Herbert Sutcliffe was on 43 when he played a ball from Australia's Bill O'Reilly on to his stumps. Remarkably the ball failed to dislodge the bails, so he was not out. Sutcliffe went on to score 194.

II

⌐ RECORD-EQUALLING ODI DEFEAT ᕀ

In December 2005, England's third one-day international against Pakistan in Karachi ended in massive defeat. Pakistan scored 353 for 6 in 50 overs, Kamran Akmal hitting his second successive century, and then took just 42 overs to bowl England out for 188. The 165-run loss equalled England's heaviest ever defeat in a one-day international. England's record margins of defeat are as follows:

165 runs	v West Indies, St Vincent	1994
165 runs	v Pakistan, Karachi	2005
162 runs	v Australia, Melbourne	1999
155 runs	v New Zealand, Wellington	2001–02
135 runs	v West Indies, Barbados	1986
10 wickets	v Sri Lanka, Colombo	2000–01
10 wickets	v Australia, Sydney	2002–03
10 wickets	v Sri Lanka, Dambulla	2003–04

⌐ MOST WICKETS IN A SERIES ᕀ

England's Sydney Barnes holds the record for taking the highest number of wickets in a Test series with 49 in four Tests during England's tour of South Africa in 1913–14. Here are the top six:

Pos.	Wickets	Player	Series & Year
1.	49 wkts (4 Tests)	Sydney Barnes (ENG)	South Africa v England, 1913/14
2.	46 wkts (5 Tests)	Jim Laker (ENG)	England v Australia, 1956
3.	44 wkts (5 Tests)	Clarrie Grimmett (AUS)	South Africa v Australia, 1935/36
4.	42 wkts (6 Tests)	Terry Alderman (AUS)	England v Australia, 1981
=5.	41 wkts (6 Tests)	Terry Alderman (AUS)	England v Australia, 1989
=5.	41 wkts (6 Tests)	Rodney Hogg (AUS)	Australia v England, 1978/79

⌐ PAYNTER IN FIFTH ᕀ

England's Eddie Paynter holds the fifth highest career Test batting average with 59.23. Paynter played in 20 Tests between 1931 and 1939, scoring four hundreds with a best of 243.

▥

⟶ DENIS COMPTON, CBE ⟞

Denis Charles Scott Compton was born on 23 May 1918 in Hendon, Middlesex. Denis and his elder brother, Leslie, played cricket against the lamp-posts at Bell Lane Elementary School. From an early age Denis's ability was there for all to see. Aged 12, he was playing for his father's team and for the North London Schools team in a match against South London Schools at Lord's, in which he made 88. Two years later, watched by Sir Pelham Warner, he made 114 at Lord's for the Elementary Schools against C.F. Tufnell's XI and led his team to a crushing victory. In 1933, the same year that he signed apprentice forms for Arsenal FC, he joined the Lord's staff and within three years he got his first game for Middlesex, aged just 18, against Sussex in the Whitsun match. Denis batted at No. 11 and scored 14 in what was an important last-wicket stand with Gubby Allen that gave Middlesex first-innings points.

By the 1930s, Compton was a leading batsman for England and played at the top of his profession during three decades. Compton was a right-handed batsman and a useful slow left-arm Chinaman bowler. In 1937 he scored 1,980 runs and was picked for England against New Zealand at The Oval, scoring 65. In his second Test for England, against Australia at Trent Bridge in 1938, he scored his first century (102) and then a match-saving 76 not out on a rain-affected pitch at Lord's which impressed even the legendary Don Bradman. Compton was just 20 years old. In 1939 he scored 2,468 runs, including 120 against the West Indies at Lord's, where he put on 248 with Len Hutton in 2 hours and 20 minutes.

In 1946, the first season after the war, Compton initially struggled but was still the leading scorer with 2,403 runs, and he made a century in each innings against Australia in Adelaide the following February. In 1947, he was England's sporting hero as he broke record after record, scoring 3,816 runs, including 18 centuries, and the incredible total of 753 runs against the touring South Africans. However, he was notoriously unreliable calling for a run, with England team-mate Trevor Bailey famously remarking that a call from Denis "should be treated as no more than a basis for negotiation."

Meanwhile Compton was also playing football. He made his Arsenal debut in 1936 and spent his entire career as a winger with the club, winning the League Championship in 1948 and the FA Cup in 1950. However, the latter part of his sporting career was dogged by knee trouble following a collision with Charlton Athletic's goalkeeper. Even so, Compton remained one of England's highest-profile sportsmen. Indeed, he was the original "Brylcreem Boy", having signed an advertising deal with the hair-care firm. Between 1951 and 1952, Compton jointly captained Middlesex CCC with Bill Edrich. Both men were later honoured with the creation of the Edrich and Compton stands at the Nursery End at Lord's.

Compton retired from cricket in 1957, having played in 78 Tests and having scored 5,807 runs, including 17 centuries, at an average of 50.06. In first-class cricket he scored 38,942 runs and 123 centuries. In retirement, he became a journalist and then a BBC television commentator. In 1991 he became the first former professional cricketer to be elected president of Middlesex CCC. Denis Compton died in 1997, aged 78.

⌐ BALDERSTONE'S DOUBLE DUTY ⌐

Chris Balderstone, who played in two Tests for England in 1976, gained the distinction of being the only man ever to play in a Football League match while scoring a County Championship century. In September 1975, he was batting for Leicestershire against Derbyshire at Chesterfield and was 51 not out when bad light stopped play midway through the evening session. With no likelihood of a resumption, Balderstone left Queen's Park and drove up to Belle Vue, the home of Doncaster Rovers FC, for whom he then played against Brentford in a Football League Division Three match. The game ended goalless and he returned to Chesterfield where, on the following morning, he completed his century, being eventually dismissed for 116.

⌐ KEEP IT IN THE FAMILY ⌐

When Kent's Dean Headley made his debut for England, he was watched by his very proud father Ron, who had been an overseas player with Worcestershire and opened the batting for the West Indies against England in two Tests in 1973. But both would no doubt admit that they were far lesser players than Ron's father, and Dean's grandfather, George Headley. Known as the "black Bradman", Headley Snr has the third highest Test batting average of all time (60.83) and was the finest batsman of the first 20 years of West Indies international cricket.

⌐ DEXTER OUTVOTED ⌐

Ted Dexter, the former Sussex and England cricketer, contested the Cardiff South East seat for the Conservatives against Labour's Jim Callaghan in the 1964 General Election. However, Dexter was unsuccessful and Callaghan went on to become Prime Minister from 1976 to 1979.

III

England, captained by Ray Illingworth, toured Australia in 1970/71, playing what was scheduled to be a six-Test series. Officially, however, the series had seven as the third Test, at Melbourne, was abandoned because of heavy rain without a ball being bowled. An additional match, which became the fifth Test, was arranged and played at the MCG after the Sydney Test. The first Test at Brisbane's Gabba had ended in a draw, as had the second at the WACA, Perth. England then won the fourth Test at the SCG to take a 1–0 lead in the series, drew the fifth Test in Melbourne and drew once again in the sixth Test at the Adelaide Oval.

England thus went back to Sydney for the seventh and final Test of the 1970/71 Ashes series with a 1–0 lead. Australia dropped their captain, Bill Lawry, promoting Ian Chappell to the captaincy. He won the toss for this six-day match and decided to field and Australia bowled England out for 184, with Ray Illingworth top-scoring on 42.

Australia in reply were 13 for 2 at the close on day one, and by stumps on the second day they had moved on to 235 for 7 (Greg Chappell 62 not out, Dennis Lillee 6 not out). They were eventually dismissed for 264, a lead of 80. However, during Australia's innings, a bouncer from John Snow hit Terry Jenner on the head, resulting in the leg-spinner being taken to hospital. At the end of the over, when Snow went to the boundary to his fielding position, a drunk grabbed his shirt and beer cans were hurled at him from the crowd. As a result Ray Illingworth took the England team from the field of play. After a short delay play resumed, but the atmosphere was extremely hostile.

England closed day three on 229 for 4, with Basil D'Oliveira on 37 not out and skipper Illingworth unbeaten on 25. When England were dismissed for 302, Australia's target to win the match, level the series and retain the Ashes was just 223. Snow broke down after bowling only two overs, but he had already dismissed opener Ken Eastwood. Six different England bowlers took wickets as the home side subsided to 160 all out, leaving England with a 62-run win and a 2–0 series victory.

Did You Know That?

Following a discussion between the Australian Cricket Board, the MCC manager and two MCC officials, the third Test in 1970/71 was abandoned as a result of poor weather just as the players were about to take the field. However, rather than disappoint the Melbourne cricket fans, the Australian Cricket Board replaced the Test with a match of 40 overs per side held at the Melbourne Cricket Ground on 5 January 1971. Australia won what is now regarded as the first ever one-day international (ODI) by 5 wickets.

III

AUSTRALIA V ENGLAND – Seventh Test

12–17 FEBRUARY 1971, SYDNEY CRICKET GROUND, AUSTRALIA

Result: England won by 62 runs. *Toss:* Australia. *Umpires:* TF Brooks, LP Rowan.

ENGLAND

JH Edrich	c GS Chappell	b Dell	30	c IM Chappell	b O'Keeffe	57
BW Luckhurst	c Redpath	b Walters	0	c Lillee	b O'Keeffe	59
KWR Fletcher	c Stackpole	b O'Keeffe	33	c Stackpole	b Eastwood	20
JH Hampshire	c Marsh	b Lillee	10	c IM Chappell	b O'Keeffe	24
BL D'Oliveira		b Dell	1	c IM Chappell	b Lillee	47
*R Illingworth		b Jenner	42	lbw	b Lillee	29
†APE Knott	c Stackpole	b O'Keeffe	27		b Dell	15
JA Snow		b Jenner	7	c Stackpole	b Dell	20
P Lever	c Jenner	b O'Keeffe	4	c Redpath	b Jenner	17
DL Underwood	not out		8	c Marsh	b Dell	0
RGD Willis		b Jenner	11		not out	2
Extras	(b 4, lb 4, w 1, nb 2)		11	(b 3, lb 3, nb 6)		12
TOTAL	(all out)		184	(all out)		302

1/5, 2/60, 3/68, 4/69, 5/98

6/145, 7/156, 8/165, 9/165, 10/184

1/94, 2/130, 3/158, 4/165, 5/234

6/251, 7/276, 8/298, 9/299, 10/302

Bowling: *First Innings:* Lillee 13–5–32–1, Dell 16–8–32–2, Walters 4–0–10–1, GS Chappell 3–0–9–0, Jenner 16–3–42–3, O'Keeffe 24–8–48–3. *Second Innings:* Lillee 14–0–43–2, Dell 26.7–3–65–3, Walters 5–0–18–0, Jenner 21–5–39–1, O'Keeffe 26–8–96–3, Eastwood 5–0–21–1, Stackpole 3–1–8–0.

AUSTRALIA

KH Eastwood	c Knott	b Lever	5		b Snow	0
KR Stackpole		b Snow	6		b Illingworth	67
†RW Marsh	c Willis	b Lever	4	(7)	b Underwood	16
*IM Chappell		b Willis	25	(3) c Knott	b Lever	6
IR Redpath	c & b	Underwood	59	(4) c Hampshire	b Illingworth	14
KD Walters	st Knott	b Underwood	42	(5) c D'Oliveira	b Willis	1
GS Chappell		b Willis	65	(6) st Knott	b Illingworth	30
KJ O'Keeffe	c Knott	b Illingworth	3	c sub (Shuttleworth)	b D'Oliveira	12
TJ Jenner		b Lever	30	c Fletcher	b Underwood	4
DK Lillee	c Knott	b Willis	6	c Hampshire	b D'Oliveira	0
AR Dell	not out		3	not out		3
Extras	(lb 5, w 1, nb 10)		16	(b 2, nb 5)		7
TOTAL	(all out)		264	(all out)		160

1/11, 2/13, 3/32, 4/66, 5/147

6/162, 7/178, 8/235, 9/239, 10/264

1/0, 2/22, 3/71, 4/82, 5/96

6/131, 7/142, 8/154, 9/154, 10/160

Bowling: *First Innings:* Snow 18–2–68–1, Lever 14.6–3–43–3, D'Oliveira 12–2–24–0, Willis 12–1–58–3, Underwood–16–3–39–2, Illingworth 11–3–16–1. *Second Innings:* Snow 2–1–7–1, Lever 12–2–23–1, D'Oliveira 5–1–15–2, Willis 9–1–32–1, Underwood 13.6–5–28–2, Illingworth 20–7–39–3, Fletcher 1–0–9–0.

Ⅲ

⁓ DUAL INTERNATIONAL SPORTSMAN ⁓

William Milton, nicknamed "Joey", represented England at rugby in 1874, winning two caps at full-back, and then moved to South Africa to join the Civil Service. Milton is one of the 11 members of the first ever sporting team to represent South Africa in international competition, some 21 years before South Africa became a united country. He was a member of the South African cricket team that played its first ever Test match at St George's Park, Port Elizabeth, on 12 and 13 March 1889. Their opponents were an England team captained by Charles Aubrey Smith. Indeed Milton, later Sir William Milton K.C.M.G., K.C.V.G., played in South Africa's first three Tests between 1889 and 1892. Sir William Milton also became the first president of the Western Province Cricket Union, served as president of the Rhodesian Rugby Union from 1900 to 1914, and was responsible for the purchase and laying-out of the grounds at the famous Harare Sports Club, which today is still a venue for international cricket in Zimbabwe. Sir William Milton also had a prominent school in Bulawayo named after him, and two of his sons carried on the family's sporting tradition and were capped for England at rugby in the early 1900s.

⁓ BOWLER TACKLES STREAKER ⁓

During the first Ashes Test against England at Perth in 1982, the Australian bowler Terry Alderman injured his shoulder while rugby-tackling a streaker. The injury resulted in him missing over a year of international cricket.

⁓ HIT THE BAR ⁓

In the fifth over of his one-day international debut for England against Bangladesh on 21 June 2005, Chris Tremlett dismissed Shahriar Nafees and Tushar Imran with consecutive deliveries. Mohammad Ashraful played defensively at the next ball, which bounced and then struck the top of the stumps. However, the bails did not fall and so Tremlett was denied a hat-trick.

⁓ DYING FOR GOLD ⁓

During the late 1880s, Sir Charles Aubrey Smith, who played one Test for England, caught pneumonia while mining for gold in South Africa and was mistakenly pronounced dead by a doctor.

III

⟿ FANTASY ENGLAND XI (8) ⟿

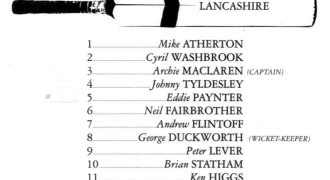

LANCASHIRE

1................................*Mike* ATHERTON
2................................*Cyril* WASHBROOK
3................................*Archie* MACLAREN *(CAPTAIN)*
4................................*Johnny* TYLDESLEY
5................................*Eddie* PAYNTER
6................................*Neil* FAIRBROTHER
7................................*Andrew* FLINTOFF
8................................*George* DUCKWORTH *(WICKET-KEEPER)*
9................................*Peter* LEVER
10................................*Brian* STATHAM
11................................*Ken* HIGGS
12th Man................................*David* LLOYD

Did You Know That?

Lancashire CCC has won the County Championship seven times (in 1897, 1904, 1926–28, 1930 and 1934) and were joint champions with Surrey in 1950. Prior to 1890, there was no official system for selecting the County Championship winners, although Lancashire claimed outright victory in 1881 and shared it in 1879, 1882 and 1889.

⟿ MARATHON MAN ⟿

Wilfred Rhodes's England Test career is the longest in history. Lasting from 1 June 1899 to 12 April 1930, a period of 30 years and 315 days, his career actually covered two centuries and five decades.

⟿ BOTHAM THE LEG-BREAKER ⟿

After hitting a double century against India in the Oval Test of 1982, Ian Botham then broke Sunil Gavaskar's shin with a square drive and put him out of the remaining matches of the visitors' tour.

⟿ ASHES FEVER (8) ⟿

"It's been my best-ever series, but unfortunately it's not been good enough."
Shane Warne, *September 2005*

Ⅲ

‒ HIGHEST ENGLAND TEST TOTALS ‒

Based on all Test matches up to and including England v Sri Lanka
at Trent Bridge, Nottingham, on Tuesday 6 June 2006.

Score	Teams	Venue	Year
903–7 dec	England v Australia	The Oval	1938
849	England v West Indies	Kingston	1929/30
658–8 dec	England v Australia	Nottingham	1938
654–5*	England v South Africa	Durban	1938/39
653–4 dec	England v India	Lord's	1990
652–7 dec	England v India	Chennai	1984/85
636	England v Australia	Sydney	1928/29
633–5 dec	England v India	Birmingham	1979
629	England v India	Lord's	1974
627–9 d	England v Australia	Manchester	1934
619–6 dec	England v West Indies	Nottingham	1957
617	England v India	Nottingham	2002
611	England v Australia	Manchester	1964
608	England v South Africa	Johannesburg	1948/49
604–9 dec	England v South Africa	The Oval	2003
595–5 dec	England v Australia	Birmingham	1985
594	England v India	The Oval	1982
593–6 dec	England v New Zealand	Auckland	1974/75
593	England v West Indies	St John's	1993/94
592–8 dec	England v Australia	Perth	1986/87
589	England v Australia	Melbourne	1911/12
583–4 dec*	England v West Indies	Birmingham	1957
580–9 dec	England v New Zealand	Christchurch	1991/92
577	England v Australia	Sydney	1903/04
576	England v Australia	The Oval	1899
571–8 dec	England v India	Manchester	1936
570–7 dec*	England v South Africa	Durban	2004/05
568	England v West Indies	Port of Spain	1967/68
568	England v West Indies	Lord's	2004
567–8 dec	England v New Zealand	Nottingham	1994
566–9 dec	England v West Indies	Birmingham	2004
564	England v India	Nottingham	1996
562–7 dec	England v New Zealand	Auckland	1962/63
560–8 dec	England v New Zealand	Christchurch	1932/33
559–9 dec	England v South Africa	Cape Town	1938/39
559–8 dec	England v India	Kanpur	1963/64
558–6 dec	England v Pakistan	Nottingham	1954

558	England v Australia	Melbourne	1965/66
554–8 dec	England v South Africa	Lord's	1947
551–6 dec	England v Sri Lanka	Lord's	2006
551	England v Australia	Sydney	1897/98
551*	England v South Africa	Nottingham	1947
550	England v New Zealand	Christchurch	1950/51
550–4 dec	England v India	Leeds	1967
548	England v Australia	Melbourne	1924/25
548–7 dec	England v New Zealand	Auckland	1932/33
546–4 dec	England v New Zealand	Leeds	1965
546–8 dec	England v Pakistan	Faisalabad	1983/84
545	England v Pakistan	The Oval	1974
545	England v Sri Lanka	Birmingham	2002
544–5 dec	England v Pakistan	Birmingham	1962
540	England v New Zealand	Auckland	1929/30
538*	England v Australia	The Oval	1975
537	England v India	Lord's	1952
537	England v West Indies	Port of Spain	1953/54
534–6 dec	England v South Africa	The Oval	1935
533	England v Australia	Leeds	1985
531–2 dec	England v South Africa	Lord's	1924
531	England v South Africa	Johannesburg	1964/65
529	England v Australia	Melbourne	1974/75
529–5 dec*	England v Sri Lanka	Lord's	2002
528–3 dec	England v Bangladesh	Lord's	2005
527	England v West Indies	The Oval	1966
526	England v New Zealand	Leeds	2004
524	England v Australia	Sydney	1932/33
521	England v Australia	Brisbane (Exhib.)	1928/29
521	England v Pakistan	Birmingham	1987
521	England v New Zealand	Auckland	1996/97
519	England v Australia	Melbourne	1928/29
519	England v India	Manchester	1990
515	England v India	The Oval	2002
512	England v Sri Lanka	Manchester	2002
507	England v Pakistan	Karachi	1961/62
505	England v South Africa	Leeds	1951
502–7	England v Pakistan	Karachi	1968/69
501	England v Australia	Adelaide	1911/12
501	England v Pakistan	Leeds	1996
500–8 d	England v India	Mumbai (BS)	1961/62

* Total scored in second innings.

III

✦ HIGHEST SUCCESSFUL ODI RUN-CHASES ✦

England appear three times in the top 16 successful run-chases in the history of one-day internationals. Unfortunately, on two of those occasions, they were the fielding team.

Total	Target	Team	Vs	Venue	Date
438–9	(435)	SA	Aus	Johannesburg	12 Mar 2006
332–8	(332)	NZ	Aus	Christchurch	10 Dec 2005
330–7	(327)	Aus	SA	Port Elizabeth	6 Apr 2002
326–8	(326)	Ind	Eng	Lord's	13 Jul 2002
325–5	(325)	Ind	WI	Ahmedabad	15 Nov 2002
319–7	(316)	Pak	Ind	Ahmedabad	12 Apr 2005
316–7	(315)	Ind	Pak	Dhaka	18 Jan 1998
316–4	(316)	Aus	Pak	Lahore	10 Nov 1998
313–6	(313)	SL	WI	Bridgetown	8 Jun 2003
313–7	(313)	SL	Zim	New Plymouth	23 Feb 1992
310–6	(305)	SA	WI	Johannesburg	4 Feb 2004
306–5	(305)	Eng	Pak	Karachi	24 Oct 2000
303–9	(303)	SL	Eng	Adelaide	23 Jan 1999
303–4	(299)	Ind	SL	Jaipur	31 Oct 2005
302–7	(302)	Ind	SA	Kochi	9 Mar 2000
300–6	(296)	Pak	SL	Kimberley	7 Apr 1998

✦ ASHES HISTORY ✦

Although England first played Australia in a Test match in 1877, it wasn't until 1882 that England and Australia were said to be playing for "the Ashes". Here are the results of their first four encounters:

1876/77	Aus 1-1 Eng	1880	**Eng** 1-0 Aus
1878/79	**Aus** 1-0 Eng	1881/82	**Aus** 2-0 Eng

✦ THE RUN-OUT THAT NEVER WAS ✦

On 21 November 2005, in the first innings of the Pakistan v England Test in Faisalabad, Inzamam-ul-Haq was declared run out after Steve Harmison threw the ball and hit the stumps at the batsman's end. However, everyone in the ground and the millions watching on television could see that Inzamam was not even attempting a run, he simply moved to one side to avoid being struck by the ball. However, Nadeem Ghauri, the third umpire, studied the evidence and, to everyone's complete and utter amazement, pressed the red light.

III

~ ENGLAND'S HONG KONG SIXERS ~

Kabir Ali ✳ Ian Blackwell ✳ Ally Brown ✳ Dougie Brown
Glen Chapple ✳ Paul Collingwood ✳ Robert Croft
Phil DeFreitas ✳ Mark Ealham ✳ John Emburey
Neil Fairbrother ✳ Andrew Flintoff ✳ Matthew Fleming
Graham Gooch ✳ Adam Hollioake ✳ Ben Hollioake
Ronnie Irani ✳ Chris Lewis ✳ Graham Lloyd ✳ Darren Maddy
Dimitri Mascarenhas ✳ Matthew Maynard ✳ Graham Napier
Dermot Reeve ✳ Chris Silverwood ✳ Gladstone Small
Robin Smith ✳ Chris Tremlett ✳ Mike Watkinson

~ OUT "OBSTRUCTING THE FIELD" ~

Sir Len Hutton of England is the only batsman to be given out "obstructing the field" in a Test match. Playing against South Africa at The Oval in 1951, he swept at a ball from off-spinner Athol Rowan. Assuming that the ball was going to strike the wicket, Hutton knocked it away and in doing so he prevented Russell Endean, the wicket-keeper, from making the catch.[†]

~ BROAD'S FURY WITH CALL ~

In England's second innings in the first Test against Pakistan in Lahore in 1987/88, Chris Broad was involved in a poor umpiring decision for the second time in a year against the same opposition. Broad pushed forward defensively to a delivery from Iqbal Qasim and despite missing the ball by inches he was given out, caught behind. Broad was furious and refused to leave the field until finally persuaded to go by his partner, Graham Gooch.

~ AND FREDDIE MAKES IT FOUR ~

Andrew Flintoff followed in the famous footsteps of Jim Laker (1956), David Steele (1975) and Ian Botham (1981), when he became only the fourth cricketer to win the BBC Sports Personality of the Year Award. His heroic performances against Australia in the 2005 Test series not only helped to regain the Ashes for England but made cricket massively popular again for the first time since Beefy's titanic Ashes performances a quarter of a century earlier.

[†]*Six years later, Russell Endean became the first Test batsman to be given out "handled the ball" during the Cape Town Test against England in 1956/57.*

Ⅲ

⌁ THE GREAT TEST MATCHES (8) ⌁

The first ever cricket match recognized as a Test match was played at the Melbourne Cricket Ground between Australia and England beginning on 15 March 1877 and was won by Australia by 45 runs. In March 1977, on their way home from a tour of India and Sri Lanka, England flew into Melbourne to celebrate the centenary of that first ever Test by playing a one-off match at the MCG. The captains for the 1977 Test were Greg Chappell and Tony Greig; the latter won the toss and put Australia in to bat.

Australia were all out for 138 in the 44th over, with their captain top-scoring with 40. By the close of play on a weather-interrupted first day, England were sitting on 29 for 1, with Mike Brearley 12 not out and nightwatchman Derek Underwood still there on 5. Bob Woolmer was the man out, having been caught by Chappell off Dennis Lillee for 9. The following day, however, the Australian pace bowlers skittled England at the cost of just a further 66 runs. Lillee was the major destructive force with 6 for 26, abetted by Max Walker with 4 for 54.

By close of play on the second day, Australia had advanced to 104 for 3 in their second innings (Ian Davis, 45, and Doug Walters, 32, steadying the Aussies after they had slipped to 53 for 3). Australia then batted throughout the third day and at the close had reached 387 for 8, with Rod Marsh 95 not out and Rick McCosker unbeaten on 17. Opener McCosker was bravely batting at number 10, having had his jaw broken by a short ball from Bob Willis in the first innings. Heavily bandaged, he eventually put on 54 with Marsh who went on to complete his century on day four in a stand that went a long way to deciding the outcome of the match.

Australia declared on 419 for 9. Chris Old was England's most successful bowler, finishing with 4 for 104. England required 463 runs to win and by close of play on the fourth day they had moved on to 191 for 2 (Derek Randall 87 not out and Dennis Amiss 34 not out). Randall went on to score a superb 174, but it wasn't enough as Lillee once again tore through the English batting order, taking 5 for 139. England went down by 45 runs, remarkably the same margin of defeat as 100 years earlier!

Did You Know That?

The opening ceremony of the 2006 Commonwealth Games took place at the Melbourne Cricket Ground on 15th March 2006. The MCG also held athletics events during the games as well as the closing ceremony on 26th March 2006.

III

AUSTRALIA V ENGLAND – Centenary Test

12–17 MARCH 1977, MELBOURNE CRICKET GROUND, AUSTRALIA

Result: Australia won by 45 runs. Toss: England. Umpires: TF Brooks, MG O'Connell

AUSTRALIA

IC Davis	lbw	b Lever	5	c Knott	b Greig	68
RB McCosker		b Willis	4	(10) c Greig	b Old	25
GJ Cosier	c Fletcher	b Lever	10	(4) c Knott	b Lever	4
*GS Chappell		b Underwood	40	(3)	b Old	2
DW Hookes	c Greig	b Old	17	(6) c Fletcher	b Underwood	56
KD Walters	c Greig	b Willis	4	(5) c Knott	b Greig	66
†RW Marsh	c Knott	b Old	28	not out		110
GJ Gilmour	c Greig	b Old	4		b Lever	16
KJ O'Keeffe	c Brearley	b Underwood	0	(2) c Willis	b Old	14
DK Lillee	not out		10	(9) c Amiss	b Old	25
MHN Walker		b Underwood	2	not out		8
Extras	(b 4, lb 2, nb 8)		14	(lb 10, nb 15)		25
TOTAL	(all out)		138	(9 wickets declared)		419

1/11, 2/13, 3/23, 4/45, 5/51

6/102, 7/114, 8/117, 9/136, 10/138

1/33, 2/40, 3/53, 4/132, 5/187

6/244, 7/277, 8/353, 9/407

Bowling:*First Innings:* Lever 12–1–36–2, Willis 8–0–33–2, Old 12–4–39–3, Underwood 11.6–2–16–3. *Second Innings:* Lever 21–1–95–2, Willis 22–0–91–0, Old 27.6–2–104–4, Greig 14–3–66–2, Underwood 12–2–38–1.

ENGLAND

RA Woolmer	c Chappell	b Lillee	9	lbw	b Walker	12
JM Brearley	c Hookes	b Lillee	12	lbw	b Lillee	43
DL Underwood	c Chappell	b Walker	7	(10)	b Lillee	7
DW Randall	c Marsh	b Lillee	4	(3) c Cosier	b O'Keeffe	174
DL Amiss	c O'Keeffe	b Walker	4	(4)	b Chappell	64
KWR Fletcher	c Marsh	b Walker	4	(5) c Marsh	b Lillee	1
*AW Greig		b Walker	18	(6) c Cosier	b O'Keeffe	41
†APE Knott	lbw	b Lillee	15	(7) lbw	b Lillee	42
CM Old	c Marsh	b Lillee	3	(8) c Chappell	b Lillee	2
JK Lever	c Marsh	b Lillee	11	(9) lbw	b O'Keeffe	4
RGD Willis	not out		1	not out		5
Extras	(b 2, lb 2, w 1, nb 2)		7	(b 8, lb 4, w 3, nb 7)		22
TOTAL	(all out)		95	(all out)		417

1/19, 2/30, 3/34, 4/40, 5/40

6/61, 7/65, 8/78, 9/86, 10/95

1/28, 2/113, 3/279, 4/290, 5/346

6/369, 7/380, 8/385, 9/410, 10/417

Bowling: *First Innings:* Lillee 13.3–2–26–6, Walker 15–3–54–4, O'Keeffe 1–0–4–0, Gilmour 5–3–4–0. *Second Innings:* Lillee 34.4–7–139–5, Walker 22–4–83–1, Gilmour 4–0–29–0, Chappell 16–7–29–1, O'Keeffe 33–6–108–3, Walters 3–2–7–0.

III

⚭ FANTASY ENGLAND XI ⚭

LEICESTERSHIRE

1. *Eddie* DAWSON
2. *Chris* BALDERSTONE
3. *David* GOWER *(CAPTAIN)*
4. *Charles* PALMER
5. *James* WHITAKER
6. *Ewart (W.E.)* ASTILL
7. *Chris* LEWIS
8. *Roger* TOLCHARD *(WICKET-KEEPER)*
9. *Ray* ILLINGWORTH
10. *Phil* DeFREITAS
11. *Ken* HIGGS
12th Man........*Darren* MADDY

Did You Know That?

Leicestershire CCC joined the County Championship in 1895, and has won it three times (1975, 1996 and 1998). The County plays its home games at Grace Road in Leicester, which is named after the legendary W.G. Grace.

⚭ ASHES FEVER (9) ⚭

"Can you put some lights on the bails? I can't see them. I don't know where I'm bowling."

Andrew Flintoff, to umpire Rudy Koertzen suggesting that the light wasn't good enough during the fifth Test of the 2005 Ashes series

⚭ TEST DEBUT HAT-TRICKS ⚭

Three players have taken a hat-trick on their Test debut: England pace bowler Maurice Allom in 1929, New Zealand off-spinner Peter Petherick in 1976, and Australian pace bowler Damien Fleming in 1994. Allom's hat-trick made up the last three of four wickets in five balls in his eighth over in Test cricket.[†]

[†] *Only two other players have taken four Test wickets in five balls: England's Chris Old against Pakistan at Edgbaston in 1978, and Pakistan's Wasim Akram against the West Indies in Lahore in 1990/91. Wasim Akram is also the only Test captain to take a hat-trick.*

III

‑⌒ SOCCER AND RUGGER OPENERS ⌒‑

When England played New Zealand at Headingley in the third Test from 5 to 9 June 1958, their innings was opened by two dual internationals. On 28 November 1951, Gloucestershire's Arthur Milton, then at Arsenal, had played in England's 2–2 draw with Austria at Wembley, and Mike (MJK) Smith of Warwickshire won one England rugby union cap, an 8–3 defeat against Wales at Twickenham, on 21 January 1956.

‑⌒ LOWEST COMPLETED TEST INNINGS ⌒‑

In the table highlighting the lowest number of runs scored by a country in an innings, five of the top six places are occupied by teams who were playing against England:

Pos.	Runs	Teams	Venue	Year
1.	26	New Zealand (v England)	Auckland	1954/55
=2.	30	South Africa (v England)	Port Elizabeth	1895/96
=2.	30	South Africa (v England)	Birmingham	1924
4.	35	South Africa (v England)	Cape Town	1898/99
=5.	36	Australia (v England)	Birmingham	1902
=5.	36	South Africa (v Australia)	Melbourne	1931/32

‑⌒ LARWOOD STICKS TO HIS PRINCIPLES ⌒‑

During the famous "Bodyline" tour of 1932/33, Harold Larwood took 33 Test wickets. However, injuries to Bill Woodfull and Bertie Oldfield from Larwood's short-pitched deliveries in Adelaide enraged the Australian public and the Australian cricketing authorities in equal measure. When Larwood returned to England, instead of being greeted as a hero, he was told to sign a letter of apology to the Australians. He refused to be made the scapegoat for "Bodyline" and was never selected to play for England again. Larwood later settled in Australia.

‑⌒ GOOCHIE'S YEAR ⌒‑

Graham Gooch enjoyed a special season in 1990, averaging 101.70 in first-class cricket. The highlight was the Lord's Test match against India, from 26 to 31 July. Gooch made the highest score ever made at Lord's (333); achieved the world record Test aggregate of 456 runs (333 and 123); became the first player ever to score a triple century and a century in the same match; it was also the highest Test score against India and the highest ever score by an England captain.

II

∽ SIR COLIN COWDREY, CBE ∽

Michael Colin Cowdrey was born in Ootacamund, Bangalore, India on 24 December 1932. Colin's father named him thus, so he would have the same initials as cricket's most famous club, the MCC. In 1946, aged just 13, he became the youngest player ever to represent his school, Tonbridge, at Lord's. Four years later he made his first-class debut for Kent, where he remained a player until his retirement in 1976. From 1952 to 1954, Cowdrey played for and captained Oxford University, and in 1956 he was made captain of Kent. In 1970 he proudly led Kent to their first County Championship since 1913.

Cowdrey made his Test debut against Australia in Brisbane during England's 1954/55 tour of Australia and New Zealand, going on to score his maiden Test century against Australia in Melbourne on Boxing Day 1954. He established himself as a world-class batsman and among his outstanding feats with the bat for England was a partnership of 411 with Peter May against the West Indies in 1957. With May ill in 1959, Cowdrey was appointed captain for the fourth and fifth Tests against India. Cowdrey went on to captain England a further 25 times, but he never achieved his ambition of leading his country in Australia: he was vice-captain for four tours down under.

In 1962 Cowdrey struck 307 against Victoria, the highest score by an MCC (England) player in Australia. A year later, against the West Indies at Lord's, Test cricket fans around the world witnessed one of the most memorable moments in the game's illustrious history. Cowdrey had made 19 in the second innings, when his arm was broken by Wes Hall. His arm was set in plaster but, when England lost their ninth wicket, he returned to the crease. Fortunately for the injured Cowdrey, David Allen faced the final four balls to rescue a nail-biting draw.

Elegant strokeplay and effortless timing brought Cowdrey 107 centuries. He briefly held the world record for Test runs in a career, before it was bettered by Garfield Sobers. Cowdrey played his 114th and final Test against Australia in 1974/75, ending his career with 7,624 Test runs. After he retired, he worked behind the scenes at Kent, became president of the MCC in 1986 and was later chairman of the International Cricket Council. In 2000, he was made president of Kent County Cricket Club. Colin Cowdrey died on 4 December 2000.

Did You Know That?

Colin Cowdrey's parents owned a tea plantation in India and he played his first cricket on a pitch cut out of the jungle. He was the first player to record centuries against all of the other Test cricket-playing nations. He scored 42,719 first-class runs in his career and took 638 catches.

⫼

⟀ BROTHERS IN ARMS ⟀

When Hanif Mohammad and his brother, Sadiq, opened the innings for Pakistan against New Zealand in 1969, it was only the second ever instance in Test cricket history of a pair of brothers opening the batting. The previous occasion had been in 1880, when E.M. and W.G. Grace opened for England.

⟀ GILMOUR'S MATCH ⟀

During the 1975 World Cup in England, Australia and England met in the semi-finals. Australian seam bowler Gary Gilmour demolished the England innings by taking 6 wickets for 14 runs from 12 overs, including 6 maidens. Unsurprisingly, it became known as "Gilmour's match", but remarkably Gilmour only played a total of five ODIs in his entire career.

⟀ THE SICK LIST ⟀

England's preparations for the first Test of their 2005/06 tour of India were thrown into disarray in the week leading up to it. On 27 February 2006, just two days before the match was due to start in Nagpur, Michael Vaughan and Simon Jones withdrew injured (they would eventually fly home, Marcus Trescothick having already returned to England home two days. England's "Sick List" was:

Ian Blackwell	Stomach complaint
Paul Collingwood	Back spasm
Simon Jones	Knee injury – flew home
Monty Panesar	Stomach complaint
Kevin Pietersen	Back injury
Liam Plunkett	Ankle injury
Matt Prior	Stomach complaint
Marcus Trescothick	Personal reasons – flew home
Shaun Udal	Stomach complaint
Michael Vaughan	Knee injury – flew home

⟀ OUT BY A NOSE ⟀

When Mike Gatting was batting against the West Indies in a one-day international at Kingston, Jamaica, in 1986, a delivery from Malcolm Marshall broke his nose. To add to his dismay the ball dropped from his nose on to the wicket and he was given out.

III

⌁ BARMY ARMY SONG (2) ⌁

Everywhere We Go
Jimmy: _Everywhere we go_
Crowd: _Everywhere we go_
The people want to know
The people want to know
Who we are
Who we are
Where we come from
Where we come from
Shall we tell them
Shall we tell them
Who we are?
Who we are?
Where we come from?
Where we come from?
We are the Army
We are the Army
The Barmy Barmy Army
The Barmy Barmy Army
We are the England
We are the England
The Mighty Mighty England
The Mighty Mighty England
Michael Vaughan's Barmy Army
Etc.

⌁ MILLENNIUM MAN AT THE DOUBLE ⌁

England's David Gower twice scored 1,000 Test runs in a calendar year. In 1982 he recorded 1,061 runs (at an average of 46.13), and in 1986 1,059 runs (at an average of 44.12).

⌁ STREAKERS AT OLD TRAFFORD ⌁

On 5 August 2002, four male streakers invaded the Old Trafford pitch during England's Test Match against the West Indies. On day three of the Test, play was continuously held up by a procession of naked males, with three of them running on to the pitch simultaneously. A fifth would-be streaker, wearing a black wig and a multi-coloured suit, then ran on to the pitch but was chased and caught by the frustrated players and officials before he could bare all.

II

~ COLLINGWOOD'S MAIDEN CENTURY ~

Paul Collingwood scored his maiden Test century (134 not out) to help England to 393 in their first innings of the First Test against India in Nagpur in March 2006. His first 50 runs came in 172 minutes from 131 balls, and included 7 fours and 1 six.[†]

~ SILVER BILLY BELDHAM ~

In 1792, five years after the MCC opened its doors for the first time, the first centuries were recorded at the original Lord's, scored by Tom Walker and "Silver Billy" Beldham. At the time a score of 110 was, for gambling purposes, considered the normal score for a whole team. Twenty-nine years after scoring his 144 for the MCC, Beldham made his final appearance for the Players against the Gentlemen in a match commemorating the coronation of George IV. In 1852, aged 86, he walked seven miles from his home in Tilford, Surrey, to watch Farncombe play an England XI. Alongside his achievements as a cricketer and an athlete, "Silver Billy" is reputed to have fathered 39 children.

~ BAD AWAY DAYS (1) ~

England's tour of France, 1789

In 1789 France was on the verge of revolution. In an attempt to allay anti-British feelings in France, the British Foreign Secretary, the Duke of Leeds, and the British Ambassador in Paris, the Duke of Dorset, a huge cricket enthusiast, organized a tour of France by a party including some of England's best cricketers. The players chosen arrived at Dover in preparation for sailing to France, only to be prevented from leaving by news that the French Revolution had begun. Meanwhile, the Duke of Dorset had already left and was due to arrive in Paris from Boulogne. History doesn't relate how he explained himself when he got to the ground!

~ PLAYER LOSES HIS ONLY TEST CAP ~

Glamorgan's prolific opening batsman Alan Jones won his one England cap against the Rest of the World in 1970, only for the cricket authorities to withdraw their recognition of these matches as Tests a few years later.

[†] *This was the first time England had played a Test match in Nagpur.*

⫿

⟿ WORLD CUP FINALS (1) ⟾

The 1979 Cricket World Cup was the second such tournament to be staged and again took place in England, between 9 and 23 June. The 1979 tournament once more had eight countries, divided into two groups of four, participating with the top two teams going into the semi-finals. Each match consisted of 60 overs per innings and the teams wore traditional white clothing. West Indies met England in the final, but looked in trouble at 99 for 4 before Viv Richards and Collis King added 139 in 77 minutes. Mike Brearley and Geoff Boycott started solidly, but slowly, in reply and England never really got close to challenging the target of 286.

ENGLAND V WEST INDIES
23 JUNE 1979, LORD'S, LONDON
Result: West Indies won by 92 runs. *Toss:* England. *Umpires:* HD Bird, BJ Meyer.

WEST INDIES			Runs	Mins	Balls	4s	6s
CG Greenidge	run out (Randall)		9	31	31	0	0
DL Haynes	c Hendrick	b Old	20	49	27	3	0
IVA Richards	not out		138	207	157	11	3
AI Kallicharran		b Hendrick	4	19	17	0	0
*CH Lloyd	c & b	Old	13	42	33	2	0
CL King	c Randall	b Edmonds	86	77	66	10	3
†DL Murray	c Gower	b Edmonds	5	12	9	1	0
AME Roberts	c Brearley	b Hendrick	0	8	7	0	0
J Garner	c Taylor	b Botham	0	4	5	0	0
MA Holding		b Botham	0	7	6	0	0
CEH Croft	not out		0	6	2	0	0
Extras	(b 1, lb 10)		11				
TOTAL	(9 wickets, 60 overs)		286				

FoW: 1/22 (Greenidge), 2/36 (Haynes), 3/55 (Kallicharran), 4/99 (Lloyd), 5/238 (King), 6/252 (Murray), 7/258 (Roberts), 8/260 (Garner), 9/272 (Holding)

Bowling	O	M	R	W
Botham	12	2	44	2
Hendrick	12	2	50	2
Old	12	0	55	2
Boycott	6	0	38	0
Edmonds	12	2	40	2
Gooch	4	0	27	0
Larkins	2	0	21	0

ENGLAND			Runs	Mins	Balls	4s	6s
*JM Brearley	c King	b Holding	64	130	130	7	0
G Boycott	c Kallicharran	b Holding	57	137	105	3	0
DW Randall		b Croft	15	36	22	0	0
GA Gooch		b Garner	32	31	28	4	0
DI Gower		b Garner	0	6	4	0	0
IT Botham	c Richards	b Croft	4	7	3	0	0
W Larkins		b Garner	0	1	1	0	0
PH Edmonds	not out		5	14	8	0	0
CM Old		b Garner	0	4	2	0	0
†RW Taylor	c Murray	b Garner	0	1	1	0	0
M Hendrick		b Croft	0	4	5	0	0
Extras	(lb 12, w 2, nb 3)		17				
TOTAL	(all out, 51 overs)		194				

FoW: 1/129 (Brearley), 2/135 (Boycott), 3/183 (Gooch), 4/183 (Gower), 5/186 (Randall), 6/186 (Larkins), 7/192 (Botham), 8/192 (Old), 9/194 (Taylor), 10/194 (Hendrick).

Bowling	O	M	R	W
Roberts	9	2	33	0
Holding	8	1	16	2
Croft	10	1	42	3
Garner	11	0	38	5
Richards	10	0	35	0
King	3	0	13	0

Did You Know That?

Graham Gooch is the only England player to have appeared in three World Cup finals.

～ DAZZLER ON THE DANCEFLOOR ～

On 17 December 2005, Darren Gough, the Essex and England fast bowler, paired with Lilya Kopylova, beat former athlete Colin Jackson and TV presenter Zoe Ball, and their respective partners, to become the first male winner of BBC1's *Strictly Come Dancing*. "I never thought I would be saying this ten weeks ago but it has been an amazing journey for a guy who has never danced," said Gough.

～ ENGLAND'S FIELDER ～

Arthur Fielder of Kent played in eight Test matches for England.

✦ THE MCC OPENS ITS DOORS ✦

In 1787, the Marylebone Cricket Club (MCC) was formed when Thomas Lord leased a stretch of land in the district of Marylebone, erected a high fence around it, built a storage shed, then made a few amendments to the surface and opened its doors for business. The club moved to its present location – Thomas Lord's third cricket ground, the modern-day Lord's – in St John's Wood, in 1814.

✦ ASHES FEVER (10) ✦

"We knew he was a very good player, but the way he has performed has been exceptional. Any side in the world would want him."
Ricky Ponting *praises Andrew Flintoff at the end of the 2005 Ashes series*

✦ TRIPLE LOSING CENTURION ✦

In 1984, England's Allan Lamb scored a century in each of three successive Tests against the West Indies. He scored 110 at Lord's, 100 at Headingley and 100 not out at Old Trafford, but ended up on the losing side in all three matches.

✦ TONY GREIG IN THE CARIBBEAN ✦

England captain Tony Greig almost sparked an international incident when he ran out Alvin Kallicharan of the West Indies during the second Test at Port of Spain, Trinidad in 1973/74. Derek Underwood bowled the last delivery of the day to Bernard Julien and when no run was scored the players began walking to the pavilion. However, the umpire, Douglas Sang Hue, had not called for time as is the law and custom, and so Greig who was fielding at silly point, picked up the ball and threw it at the stumps at the bowler's end. As soon as Greig's throw hit the stumps and knocked off the bails, he appealed for a dismissal and Sang Hue gave it. By the time the crowds got home news had spread that Kallicharan had actually been given out. However, overnight England agreed that Kallicharan should be reinstated even though he was legally out within the laws of the game.

✦ ALL-ROUND PERFORMANCE ✦

In the 1920/21 Ashes series against England Jack Gregory, the Australian all-rounder, took 23 wickets, averaged over 70 with the bat and also took 15 catches.

III

FANTASY ENGLAND XI (10)

MIDDLESEX

1	*Andrew* STRAUSS
2	*Jack* ROBERTSON
3	*Denis* COMPTON
4	*Bill* EDRICH
5	*Mike* GATTING *(CAPTAIN)*
6	*Patsy* HENDREN
7	*John* MURRAY *(WICKET-KEEPER)*
8	*Fred* TITMUS
9	*Angus* FRASER
10	*Gubby* ALLEN
11	*Phil* TUFNELL
12th Man	*Peter* PARFITT

Did You Know That?
Middlesex CCC is named after the historic county of Middlesex and the County plays its home games at what many regard as the home of cricket, Lord's. Middlesex have won the County Championship 10 times (1903, 1920, 1921, 1947, 1976, 1980, 1982, 1985, 1990 and 1993) and shared it twice, with Yorkshire in 1949 and with Kent in 1977.

ENGLAND HOST THREE ICC TROPHIES

England hosted the first three ICC Trophy competitions. Past winners of the competition are as follows:

Year	Hosts	Winners	Runners-up	Won by
1979	England	Sri Lanka	Canada	60 runs
1982	England	Zimbabwe	Bermuda	5 wkts
1986	England	Zimbabwe	Netherlands	25 runs
1990	Netherlands	Zimbabwe*	Netherlands	6 wkts
1994	Kenya	Namibia	Denmark	41 runs
1997	Malaysia	Bangladesh	Kenya	2 wkts
2001	Canada	Netherlands	Namibia	2 wkts
2005	Ireland	Scotland	Ireland	47 runs

Following their third consecutive victory in the tournament, Zimbabwe was given full ICC member status.

III

INDIA'S DISASTROUS 1974 TOUR

In 1974 England exacted revenge over India for their 1–0 Test series defeat three years earlier by beating the visitors 3–0. Things went badly for India as soon as they arrived in England. Firstly, their captain, Ajit Wadekar, had a very ugly and public war of words with Bishan Bedi; secondly, Indian opener Sudhir Naik was accused of stealing a pair of socks from Marks & Spencer's; thirdly, England bowled India out at Lord's for a ground-record low score of 42; and, fourthly, a row took place at the residence of the Indian High Commissioner, where the Indian team were shown the door after being unavoidably late to a function as a result of heavy traffic in London. The Indian Commissioner later relented, and allowed the team back in. Finally, at the end of the tour, Bedi was banned by the Board of Cricket Control for India (BCCI) from the first Test in India's next home Test series against the West Indies on account of having given an "unauthorized" interview on British television.

TOP 5 TEST MATCH BOWLING RETURNS

Two England bowlers occupy the top two places in the list of the five best bowling figures in a Test match:

Pos.	Figures	Player	Match	Venue	Year
1.	19–90	Jim Laker	England v Australia	Manchester	1956
2.	17–159	Sydney Barnes	England v South Africa	Johannesburg	1913/14
3.	16–136	Narendra Hirwani	India v West Indies	Chennai	1987/88
4.	16–137	Bob Massie	Australia v England	Lord's, London	1972
5.	16–220	Muttiah Muralitharan	Sri Lanka v England	The Oval	1998

SIX AND OUT

In 1611 two men were prosecuted for playing cricket instead of going to church in the Sussex village of Sidlesham, just south of Chichester. In 1622 six cricketers were brought before a church tribunal by wardens in nearby Boxgrove, just north of Chichester, for profaning the Sabbath and because they broke church windows with their cricket ball.

II

⟶ LAKER SCOOPS BBC AWARD ⟶

In 1956 Jim Laker won the third BBC Sports Personality of the Year Award. In the 1956 Ashes Test at Old Trafford, Laker took 9 Australian wickets for 37 in the first innings and 10 for 53 in the second, giving him world record match figures of 19 wickets for 90 runs. He also took 10 Australian wickets in an innings for Surrey.

⟶ THE WALTER LAWRENCE TROPHY ⟶

In 1934 cricket enthusiast Walter Lawrence, a builder by trade, introduced the Walter Lawrence Trophy. It is presented annually to the cricketer who scores the fastest century in English first-class cricket. The award is currently based on the number of balls received, including no balls, but not wides – which, by definition, cannot be reached. In addition, a century scored against "declaration bowling", when non-regular bowlers feed batsmen runs to set up a run chase, is not eligible. When Frank Woolley of Kent won the inaugural trophy, the criterion was the actual time taken to score a century as opposed to today's number of balls faced rule. When Sir Walter died in 1939, the trophy was not awarded for a number of years. However, in 1966 Brian Thornton, Sit Walter's grandson-in-law, resurrected the trophy, but based on balls faced. In 1971 the original time criterion was reintroduced, but in 1985 – with slow over rates creating a somewhat uneven competition – it was decided that the trophy should, once again, be decided in terms of the number of balls faced rather than time spent at the crease. Here are the last five winners:

Year/Player	No. of balls	For	Against	Ground
2001				
Ian Harvey	61	Gloucestershire	Derbyshire	Bristol
2002				
Matthew Fleming	66	Kent	Sri Lanka	Canterbury
2003				
Damien Martyn	65	Yorkshire	Gloucestershire	Leeds
2004				
Richard Johnson	63	Somerset	Durham.	Chester-le-Street
2005				
Ian Blackwell	67	Somerset	Derbyshire	Taunton

Did You Know That?
Blackwell's score of 107 included 2 sixes and 18 fours.

III

◦ ANDREW FLINTOFF, MBE ◦

Andrew "Freddie" Flintoff was born on 6 December 1977 in Preston. Following his talismanic performances for England against Australia during the 2005 Ashes series he became widely regarded as one of the world's best all-rounders. After representing his local club, Harris Park, Andrew joined St Annes Cricket Club, aged 13. During his three years with St Annes, he impressed everyone with his aggressive bowling and hard-hitting batting. In 1993 Lancashire came knocking on Andrew's door. His first-class debut came in 1995, when he was just 17, but, in a side captained by Michael Atherton, he scored just seven runs and dropped several catches. In 1996, he was given the captaincy of the England Under-19 side that went to Pakistan in the winter and entertained Zimbabwe at home the following summer.

Flintoff hit the headlines in June 1998, when he struck Surrey's Alex Tudor for 34 in a single over in a County Championship match at Old Trafford. The following month, Freddie made his Test debut against South Africa, scoring 17 runs and taking two wickets. Although he continued to play some destructive innings, such as his 66-ball 143 against Essex in 1999 and an 111-ball 135 not out against Surrey in 2000, Flintoff's career still had not properly taken off. In 2000 he was taken to task over his weight, responding with 42 not out from just 45 balls in a ODI against Zimbabwe, for which he was named Man of the Match. "Not bad for a fat lad," Freddie quipped on receiving his award.

Nevertheless, Flintoff lost his place in the England team in 2001, and with question marks remaining over his fitness he attended the ECB National Academy that winter. Revitalised, he was called into the England squad that was touring India. He struggled with the bat against Indian spinners, but his bowling won him a Man of the Match award in the Test at Bangalore. Then in the final one-day international, he was asked to bowl the final over with India needing just 11 runs to claim victory. Flintoff first ran out Anil Kumble and then bowled Javagal Srinath in successive balls to give England the win. At the end of the game he ripped off his shirt in a display of pent up frustration and elation in equal measure.

Freddie's maiden Test century came soon after, against New Zealand in the first match of the 2001/02 series at Christchurch. He followed this up by notching a century and three fifties in the home series against South Africa. After excelling on England's tour of the West Indies in 2003/04 he was named one of *Wisden*'s Cricketers of the Year in 2004. During England's historic 2005 Ashes win over Australia he broke Ian Botham's 1981 record of six sixes in an Ashes Test by striking nine massive hits against the Aussie bowling in the second Test, and was named England's Man of the Series.

In October 2005, Flintoff shared the ICC's Sir Garfield Sobers Trophy for the world's leading cricketer with South Africa's Jacques Kallis and then in December that year he won the BBC Sports Personality of the Year Award. Freddie began 2006 with further celebration as he was awarded the MBE in the New Year's Honours List, and in March 2006, he took over as captain of England on their tour of India when Michael Vaughan was injured.

‑⚬ LOWEST EVER TEST MATCH INNINGS ⚬‑

On 28 March 1955, in the second and final Test match of a brief series at Eden Park, Auckland, New Zealand wrapped up England's first innings for 246, giving the tourists a lead of 46. Amazingly, it was enough of an advantage for England to claim an innings victory because they bowled out New Zealand for just 26 runs in only 106 minutes. The innings lasted 27 overs as Ron Appleyard took four wickets, Brian Statham three, Frank Tyson two and Johnny Wardle the other. Three New Zealanders bagged pairs, being dismissed for a duck in both innings: Matt Poore, Ian Colquhoun and Johnny Hayes. The Kiwis slumped from 22 for 5 to 26 all out, to finish up with the lowest score in Test cricket by four runs, South Africa having been dismissed for 30 by England on two occasions. Strangely, the match aggregate – 472 for 30 wickets – is not in the 20 lowest totals for a completed Test match.

‑⚬ FIRST AND LAST TEST HAT-TRICKS ⚬‑

The first Test cricket hat-trick was achieved by Australia's Fred Spofforth when he dismissed three England batsmen with consecutive deliveries on 2 January 1879 at the Melbourne Cricket Ground, Australia. It was only the third Test match in history. Up to the end of October 2005, a Test hat-trick had been achieved 35 times since the first Test match in 1877. The most recent Test hat-trick was taken by the New Zealand pace bowler James Franklin on 20 October 2004.[†]

[†]*Only one player has taken two hat-tricks in the same Test match. Jimmy Matthews played for Australia against South Africa at Old Trafford in the first match of the 1912 Triangular Tournament. The Triangular Tournament involved Australia, England and South Africa. Matthews took a hat-trick in each of South Africa's innings on 28 May.*

III

⟶ THE GREAT TEST MATCHES (9) ⟵

The third Test of the 1981 Ashes series in England took place from 16 to 21 July at Headingley in Leeds. Prior to Australia's 1981 tour, much of the cricket talk had been about skipper Greg Chappell's decision not to travel after leading his country in 33 Tests, a move which led to the return of vice-captain Kim Hughes to the top job.

England were 1–0 down in the series after losing at Trent Bridge and drawing at Lord's. Key all-rounder Ian Botham, seemingly at a low ebb after bagging a pair at Lord's, had resigned as England captain, being replaced as skipper by his predecessor Mike Brearley. Australia won the toss and after Hughes took Dennis Lillee and Rodney Marsh to re-inspect the wicket, he decided to bat first. Hughes had previously asked the veteran Australian broadcaster Alan McGilvray to inspect the wicket a couple of hours earlier and he had advised Hughes against batting last.

By the close of play on the first day Australia were 203 for 3 (Hughes 24, Ray Bright 1). Opening batsman John Dyson had made an excellent 102 before being bowled by Graham Dilley. Australia declared late on the second day, on 401 for 9 (Botham 6 for 95), leaving England a tricky, short period of play up to the close. They negotiated it safely, reaching 7 for 0 (Graham Gooch 2, Geoffrey Boycott 0). The following day, however, England succumbed for just 174 (Botham top-scoring with 50). Hughes quickly enforced the follow-on and, by the end of day three, a demoralized England were 6 for 1 in their second innings, Gooch having fallen to Lillee, caught by Terry Alderman, for a duck.

England slipped to 105 for 5 and then 135 for 7 and were staring defeat in the face, needing another 92 to avoid an innings defeat. However, cometh the hour, cometh the man, and up stepped Botham to take control of the match and inscribe his name indelibly in the English cricket history books. Botham took on the Australian bowling attack, ably supported by Graham Dilley (whose 56 came in a partnership of 117) and Chris Old (29 out of 67), enabling England to end the fourth day on 351 for 9. The last pair were eventually separated with England on 356, Bob Willis contributing two to a partnership of 37. Botham ended up 149 not out from 148 balls.

Australia required 130 to win, but Willis ripped through their batting, taking 8 for 43 and reducing the tourists to 111 all out. England had recorded a remarkable Test victory. It was the first time since 1894 and only the second time ever that England had won a Test match after being forced to follow on. Bookmakers were offering 500/1 against an England victory when the score was 135/7.

▓▓

ENGLAND V AUSTRALIA – Third Test
16–21 JULY 1981, HEADINGLEY, LEEDS
Result: England by 18 runs. *Toss:* Australia. *Umpires:* DGL Evans, BJ Meyer.

AUSTRALIA

J Dyson		b Dilley	102	c Taylor	b Willis	34
GM Wood	lbw	b Botham	34	c Taylor	b Botham	10
TM Chappell	c Taylor	b Willey	27	c Taylor	b Willis	8
*KJ Hughes	c & b	Botham	89	c Botham	b Willis	0
RJ Bright		b Dilley	7	(8)	b Willis	19
GN Yallop	c Taylor	b Botham	58	(5) c Gatting	b Willis	0
AR Border	lbw	b Botham	8	(6)	b Old	0
†RW Marsh		b Botham	28	(7) c Dilley	b Willis	4
GF Lawson	c Taylor	b Botham	13	c Taylor	b Willis	1
DK Lillee	not out		3	c Gatting	b Willis	17
TM Alderman	not out		0	not out		0
Extras	(b 4, lb 13, w 3, nb 12)		32	(lb 3, w 1, nb 14)		18
TOTAL	(for 9 wickets declared)		401	(all out)		111

1/55, 2/149, 3/196, 4/220, 5/332
6/354, 7/357, 8/396, 9/401

1/13, 2/56, 3/58, 4/58, 5/65
6/68, 7/74, 8/75, 9/110, 10/111

Bowling: *First Innings:* Willis 30–8–72–0, Old 43–14–91–0, Dilley 27–4–78–2, Botham 39.2–11–95–6, Willey 13–2–31–1, Boycott 3–2–2–0. *Second Innings:* Willis 15.1–3–43–8, Old 9–1–21–1, Dilley 2–0–11–0, Botham 7–3–14–1, Willey 3–1–4–0.

ENGLAND

GA Gooch	lbw	b Alderman	2	c Alderman	b Lillee	0
G Boycott		b Lawson	12	lbw	b Alderman	46
*JM Brearley	c Marsh	b Alderman	10	c Alderman	b Lillee	14
DI Gower	c Marsh	b Lawson	24	c Border	b Alderman	9
MW Gatting	lbw	b Lillee	15	lbw	b Alderman	1
P Willey		b Lawson	8	c Dyson	b Lillee	33
IT Botham	c Marsh	b Lillee	50	not out		149
†RW Taylor	c Marsh	b Lillee	5	c Bright	b Alderman	1
GR Dilley	c & b	Lillee	13		b Alderman	56
CM Old	c Border	b Alderman	0		b Lawson	29
RGD Willis	not out		1	c Border	b Alderman	2
Extras	(b 6, lb 11, w 6, nb 11)		34	(b 5, lb 3, w 3, nb 5)		16
TOTAL	(all out)		174	(all out)		356

1/12, 2/40, 3/42, 4/84, 5/87
6/112, 7/148, 8/166, 9/167, 10/174

1/0, 2/18, 3/37, 4/41, 5/105
6/133, 7/135, 8/252, 9/319, 10/356

Bowling: *First Innings:* Lillee 18.5–7–49–4, Alderman 19–4–59–3, Lawson 13–3–32–3.
Second Innings: Lillee 25–6–94–3, Alderman 35.3–6–135–6, Lawson 23–49–6–1, Bright 4–0–15–0.

II

⁓ FANTASY ENGLAND XI (11) ⁓

NORTHAMPTONSHIRE

1	*Raman* SUBBA ROW
2	*Colin* MILBURN
3	*Allan* LAMB
4	*David* STEELE
5	*Freddie* BROWN *(CAPTAIN)*
6	*Peter* WILLEY
7	*David* CAPEL
8	*Keith* ANDREW *(WICKET-KEEPER)*
9	*David* LARTER
10	*Nick* COOK
11	*Frank* TYSON
12th Man	*Nick* COOK

Did You Know That?

Northamptonshire CCC is considered to be the oldest club in the present-day County Championship, having been formed in 1820 before being considerably restructured in 1878. In 1904, the county applied for first-class status and was promoted the following year. Northamptonshire are one of only four counties that have never won the County Championship.

⁓ GOOCH THE SELECTOR ⁓

In 1996 Graham Gooch was appointed an England selector and held that position for four seasons. In 2002 he was appointed the head coach of Essex, and in 2005 he accepted a wider role within the club. He also started the Graham Gooch Scholarship Fund, an initiative to raise money to send some of Essex's best young professionals on overseas scholarships.

⁓ DUCKLESS ASHES INNINGS ⁓

John Edrich played 57 Test innings against Australia without ever being out for a duck. Meanwhile, Australia's Charlie Macartney is the only distinguished Australian Test cricket batsman to finish his Ashes career against England without registering a duck. Macartney played 42 innings.

Ⅲ

~ THE NAWAB OF PATAUDI ~

Iftikhar Ali Khan (the Nawab of Pataudi) is one of only a few cricketers to have played for two countries. Indeed, he is the only Test cricketer to have played for both England and India. He attended Oxford University and in 1929 won a Blue, saving the match against Cambridge with scores of 106 and 84. In 1931, topped the Oxford University averages with 1,307 runs at 93. During that summer, Cambridge University's A. Ratcliffe scored 201 against Oxford to set a new record for the Varsity Match. Pataudi immediately declared that he would beat Ratcliffe's record score, and the following day he did, hitting 238 not out. This new Varsity Match record stood until 2005. Following in the famous footsteps of Ranjitsinhji and Duleepsinhji, Pataudi scored a century for England in the first Test of the 1932/33 Ashes series; it was also his Test debut. However, he was dropped after the second Test for criticizing the England captain Douglas Jardine's use of the infamous bodyline tactics. Pataudi was appointed captain of India for their 1936 tour of England but later withdrew. Ten years later he captained the Indian cricket team that toured England in 1946. In total he played in six Tests for England during his time with Worcestershire. He was also a fine billiards and hockey player and an accomplished after-dinner speaker. His son Mansur Ali (the next Nawab of Pataudi), also played cricket for Oxford University and then county cricket for Sussex. He later captained the Indian cricket team – a father and son feat without parallel in India.

~ BEEFY STRONGARMS AUSSIES ~

On 5th March 1992, Ian Botham took 4 for 31 runs and scored 53 against Australia to earn himself the Man of the Match award in England's 8-wicket win over the home nation at the Sydney Cricket Ground during the 1992 World Cup.

~ RHODES BREAKS RECORDS ~

In Sydney during the 1903/04 Ashes series, Wilfred Rhodes came in to bat for England at No. 11 and proceeded to play a magnificent part in one of the greatest last-wicket partnerships of all time. Along with Tip Foster he added 130 for the tenth wicket, which is still a record for England today, Rhodes's own score being 40 not out. Eight years later Rhodes went in first for England along with Jack Hobbs at Melbourne and they produced a record-breaking first-wicket stand of 323.

III

↶ PAKISTAN'S HISTORIC WIN ↷

In 1954, Pakistan arrived in England for their first ever Test series on English soil and went home as the first side to win a Test on their maiden visit to England. It was a very wet summer, and the first and third Tests were affected by rain, both ending as draws. In the second Test at Trent Bridge England won easily by an innings and 129 runs thanks to a double century (278) from Denis Compton. However, Pakistan's moment of glory came in the fourth and final Test at The Oval. England looked set for victory when Pakistan were all out for 133 in their first innings, with Frank Tyson taking 4 for 35. But Pakistan's fast bowlers struck back and bowled England out for 130, with Fazal Mahmood and Mahmood Hussain sharing the England wickets. In the second innings Pakistan struggled again but still managed a score of 164, with Johnny Wardle taking 7 for 35. This left England needing only 168 runs to win, and at 109 for 2 they were on course to clinch the series. However, after Peter May fell for 53 and Compton for 29, England's middle order and tail collapsed and England were all out for 143, giving Pakistan a 24-run victory. Just as he did in the first innings, Fazal Mahmood took 6 wickets (6–30), and thus Pakistan became the first side to win a Test match in their first rubber in England.

↶ BEEFY IS BBC'S SPORTS PERSONALITY ↷

In 1981 Ian Botham followed in the footsteps of Jim Laker (1956) and David Steele (1975), becoming only the third cricketer to win the BBC Sports Personality of the Year Award. His century for England against Australia in the third Test at Headingley in 1981 remains one of the greatest counter-attacking innings in the history of cricket.

↶ ENGLAND CRICKETERS IN LIBEL CASE ↷

In 1996 Imran Khan, the former Pakistan cricket captain, now a politician, hired Mr George Carman QC to defend him in a libel case that had been brought against him by England cricketing legends Ian Botham and Allan Lamb. Both Botham and Lamb sued Khan over an *India Today* interview in which Imran allegedly accused them of racism, being uneducated and lacking class and upbringing. In a separate action Botham also sued Imran for libel after the former Pakistan player claimed that illegal ball tampering was commonplace among fast bowlers. The jury found in favour of Imran in both actions.

III

ASHES FEVER (11)

"I thought the Ashes were important, but I didn't realise how important until I saw the number of people who turned out today. It was surreal and very emotional on the bus."

Michael Vaughan, *reflecting on the day after the series ended and the open-top bus ride through London*

BAILEY'S OLD TRAFFORD HEROICS

England all-rounder Trevor Bailey had many reasons to be fond of Old Trafford, but unlike almost all of his international cricketing counterparts, he was once part of an historic game at the other Old Trafford, the home of Manchester United. In 1952/53, United were the defending Football League champions, while Bailey was a half-back for Walthamstow Avenue, the amateur champions of England. Amazingly the two champion sides were drawn together in the third round of the FA Cup, United having home advantage. The result at Old Trafford? Manchester United 1, Walthamstow Avenue 1. There were a few shocks in the replay, played in front of more than 50,000 at Highbury (the Avenue's Green Pond Road stadium, even though it was palatial by amateur standards, had a capacity of barely 12,500), but United eventually prevailed 5–2.

ENGLAND'S APPLEYARD

Yorkshire bowler Bob Appleyard played in nine Tests for England between 1954 and 1956, taking 31 wickets at an average of 17.87. When Surrey's Alf Gover died on 7 October 2001, Appleyard became the sole survivor of the 28 bowlers to have taken 200 or more first-class wickets in an English cricket season, a feat that Appleyard achieved in 1951, in his first full season, at the remarkable average of 14.14.

COWDREY THE PRANKSTER

Colin Cowdrey was, by his own admission, no athlete as a fielder, but he was an exceptional slip catcher, who possessed one of the safest pairs of hands in English cricket history. On the field he also enjoyed pulling the occasional practical joke. During one match, he took a smart catch, pocketed the ball in almost one movement and turned as if to look for it. The ruse completely confused his teammates and the umpires, too, as they had missed his sleight of hand.

Ⅲ

~ ENGLAND'S LOWEST TEST TOTALS ~

Based on all matches up to and including England v Sri Lanka, third
Test at Trent Bridge, Nottingham, June 2006.

Score	Teams	Venue	Year
45	England v Australia	Sydney	1886/87
46	England v West Indies	Port of Spain	1993/94
52	England v Australia	The Oval	1948
53	England v Australia	Lord's	1888
61	England v Australia	Melbourne	1901/02
61	England v Australia	Melbourne	1903/04
62	England v Australia	Lord's	1888
64	England v New Zealand	Wellington	1977/78
65	England v Australia	Sydney	1894/95
71	England v West Indies	Manchester	1976
72	England v Australia	Sydney	1894/95
75	England v Australia	Melbourne	1894/95
76	England v South Africa	Leeds	1907
77	England v Australia	The Oval	1882
77	England v Australia	Sydney	1884/85
77	England v Australia	Lord's	1997
79	England v Australia	Brisbane	2002/03
82	England v New Zealand	Christchurch	1983/84
84	England v Australia	The Oval	1896
87	England v Australia	Leeds	1909
87	England v Australia	Melbourne	1958/59
89	England v West Indies	Birmingham	1995
92	England v South Africa	Cape Town	1898/99
92	England v Australia	Melbourne	1994/95
93	England v New Zealand	Christchurch	1983/84
93	England v West Indies	Manchester	1988
95	England v Australia	Manchester	1884
95	England v Australia	Melbourne	1976/77
99	England v Australia	Sydney	1901/02
99	England v South Africa	Lord's	1994

~ CONFUSION REIGNS ~

During the Test match between England and Australia in Sydney
in December 1979, Geoff Boycott confused both the match scorers
and the umpires when he took strike at the wrong end, following an
interval for drinks!

II

⌒ MOST RUNS IN AN INNINGS ⌒

Sri Lanka heads the table for scoring the highest number of runs in
a Test innings with 952 for 6 declared. However, England occupies
second and third places:

Pos. Runs	Teams	Venue	Year
1. 952–6 d	Sri Lanka (v India)	Colombo	1997
2. 903–7 d	England (v Australia)	The Oval, London	1938
3. 849	England (v West Indies)	Kingston	1929/30
4. 790–3 d	West Indies (v Pakistan)	Kingston	1957/58
5. 758–8 d	Australia (v West Indies)	Kingston	1954/55

⌒ STEWARD HURT IN PITCH INVASION ⌒

In June 2001, a steward suffered a broken rib and a damaged spleen
following a pitch invasion by Pakistan supporters during England's
one-day international against Pakistan at Headingley.

⌒ AN UNUSUAL DISMISSAL ⌒

In the third Test against Pakistan at Headingley in 1987, England
opener Chris Broad was given out in unusual circumstances to the
second ball of the second innings. Broad shaped to let the delivery
from Imran Khan go through outside his off stump, but as he
withdrew his hand from the bat handle the ball deflected off his
glove, which by this point was well clear of the bat. The law was on
Broad's side and the replays showed that he was clearly not out, but
the umpire, David Shepherd, sent him back to the pavilion. Imran
Khan ended the innings with 7 for 40, as Pakistan won comfortably
by an innings and 18 runs.

⌒ KUMAR DULEEPSINHJI ⌒

Kumar Shri Duleepsinhji was born on 13 June 1905 in Kathiawar,
one of India's princely states. Like his uncle, Kumar Shri Ranjitsinhji,
Duleep came to England and played cricket for Sussex and England.
He made his England debut in the first Test against South Africa
at Edgbaston in 1929 and represented England for the last time in
1931, in the third Test against New Zealand at Old Trafford. He
scored 995 Test runs at an average of 58.52. He died in Bombay
(now Mumbai) on 5th December 1959. India's Duleep Trophy is
named in his honour.

III

∽ WORLD CUP FINALS (2) ∾

The 1987 Cricket World Cup was the fourth to be staged, but whereas the first three were all played in England, the 1987 tournament was co-hosted by India and Pakistan. It took place between 9 October and 8 November. The format was the same as for the 1983 competition apart from a reduction in the number of overs per innings, from 60 to 50. Eight countries took part in the tournament with the preliminary matches being played in two groups of four, each country playing the three other teams in its group twice. In the final against England, the Australians batted first and got off to a good start with 52 from the first ten overs against some wayward bowling. England managed to peg the Aussies back, only for their last six overs to go for 65 as Allan Border and Mike Veletta cut loose. Despite the early loss of Tim Robinson, England's reply was coming along nicely when Mike Gatting attempted a reverse sweep off Border's first ball and was caught behind. The incident turned the match despite a late flurry from Phil DeFreitas.

ENGLAND V AUSTRALIA
8 NOVEMBER 1987, EDEN GARDENS, CALCUTTA, INDIA
Result: Australia won by 7 runs. *Toss:* Australia. *Umpires:* RB Gupta and Mahboob Shah.

AUSTRALIA			Runs	Mins	Balls	4s	6s
DC Boon	c Downton	b Hemmings	75	159	125	7	0
GR Marsh		b Foster	24	71	49	3	0
DM Jones	c Athey	b Hemmings	33	75	57	1	1
CJ McDermott		b Gooch	14	6	8	2	0
*AR Border	run out (Robinson/Downton)		31	48	31	3	0
MRJ Veletta	not out		45	50	31	6	0
SR Waugh	not out		5	5	4	0	0
Extras	(b 1, lb 13, w 5, nb 7)		26				
TOTAL	(5 wickets, 50 overs)		253				

DidNot Bat: SP O'Donnell, +GC Dyer, TBA May, BA Reid.

FoW: 1/75 (Marsh), 2/151 (Jones), 3/166 (McDermott), 4/168 (Boon), 5/241 (Border).

Bowling	O	M	R	W
DeFreitas	6	1	34	0
Small	6	0	33	0
Foster	10	0	38	1
Hemmings	10	1	48	2
Emburey	10	0	44	0
Gooch	8	1	42	1

ENGLAND			*Runs*	*Mins*	*Balls*	*4s*	*6s*
GA Gooch	lbw	b O'Donnell	35	74	57	4	0
RT Robinson	lbw	b McDermott	0	2	1	0	0
CWJ Athey	run out (Waugh/Reid)		58	126	103	2	0
*MW Gatting	c Dyer	b Border	41	55	45	3	1
AJ Lamb		b Waugh	45	56	55	4	0
†PR Downton	c O'Donnell b Border		9	13	8	1	0
JE Emburey	run out (Boon/McDermott)		10	27	16	0	0
PAJ DeFreitas	c Reid	b Waugh	17	10	10	2	1
NA Foster	not out		7	12	6	0	0
GC Small	not out		3	6	3	0	0
Extras	(b 1, lb 14, w 2, nb 4)		21				
TOTAL	(8 wickets, 50 overs)		246				

Did Not Bat: EE Hemmings.

FoW: 1/1 (Robinson), 2/66 (Gooch), 3/135 (Gatting), 4/170 (Athey), 5/188 (Downton), 6/218 (Emburey), 7/220 (Lamb), 8/235 (DeFreitas).

Bowling	*O*	*M*	*R*	*W*
McDermott	10	1	51	1
Reid	10	0	43	0
Waugh	9	0	37	2
O'Donnell	10	1	35	1
May	4	0	27	0
Border	7	0	38	2

‑ CROWD APPEASED BY ENGLAND ‑

On 27th January 1985, England played an ODI match for the first time at the Sector 16 Stadium, Chandigarh, India. However, prior to play a violent thunderstorm flooded the ground. In order to placate the 25,000 crowd a game of 15 overs' duration was staged in almost unplayable conditions. England won by 7 runs and the series 4–1.

‑ WE'VE GOT YOU LICKED ‑

In 1973, Britain issued its first postage stamps depicting a cricketer. Who else but the legendary Dr W.G. Grace was on the tip of everyone's tongues.

Did You Know That?
W.G. Grace trained in medicine at St Bart's Hospital in London.

Ⅲ

～ BAD AWAY DAYS (2) ～

MCC "A" team tour to Pakistan, 1955/56

More than three decades before Mike Gattting's infamous bust-up with umpire Shakoor Rana, English cricketers found themselves in a clash of cultures in Pakistan. During the third unofficial Test in Peshawar, some of the MCC players gave Idris Begh, a local umpire, a friendly drenching with cold water. Several of the MCC players had already made a few undiplomatic remarks following a number of leg-before decisions that failed to go their way, and the incident, which was meant as a good-natured joke, was interpreted by some as a malicious attack on the umpire. The controversy spiralled out of control, resulting in Lord Alexander, the President of the MCC, offering to recall the team. His offer was declined, but the atmosphere was somewhat tainted during the remaining matches of the tour.

～ THE BEDSER TWINS ～

Sir Alec Bedser and his brother Eric were identical twins. Alec was a fast-medium bowler who was one of England's greatest Test players. Eric was a high-class spin bowler in county cricket. The story goes that when the two boys were at school, they tossed a coin to decide which one of them would become a pace bowler and which would become a spinner. Alec won and chose to be a pace bowler.

～ THREE AGAINST THREE ～

In 1743, "Three of England" played against "Three of Kent" for a wager of 500 guineas at the Artillery Ground in Finsbury. An estimated 10,000 people turned up to watch, including the Prince of Wales and other notable figures in British society at the time.

～ ASIAN AND BLACK CRICKETERS ～

Kumar Shri Ranjitsinhji ✣ Kumar Shri Duleepsinhji
Gladstone Small ✣ Devon Malcolm ✣ Mark Ramprakash
David Lawrence ✣ Neil Williams ✣ Owais Shah ✣ Roland Butcher
Philip DeFreitas ✣ Usman Afzaal ✣ Joey Benjamin
Nasser Hussain ✣ Iftikhar Ali Khan (the Nawab of Pataudi)
Min Patel ✣ Wilf Slack ✣ Kabir Ali
Vikram Solanki ✣ Raman Subba Row ✣ Alex Tudor
Norman Cowans ✣ Chris Lewis ✣ Monte Lynch ✣ Monty Panesar
Aftab Habib ✣ Sajid Mahmood

FANTASY ENGLAND XI (12)

NOTTINGHAMSHIRE

1	*Tim* ROBINSON
2	*Chris* BROAD
3	*Reg* SIMPSON
4	*Arthur* SHREWSBURY *(CAPTAIN)*
5	*Derek* RANDALL
6	*George* GUNN
7	*Bruce* FRENCH *(WICKET-KEEPER)*
8	*Alfred* SHAW
9	*Harold* LARWOOD
10	*Eddie* HEMMINGS
11	*Bill* VOCE
12th Man	*Usman* AFZAAL

Did You Know That?

Nottinghamshire CCC's Trent Bridge ground is a regular venue for Test match cricket. Nottinghamshire have won the County Championship five times (1907, 1929, 1981, 1987 and 2005) and were the winners of the second division of the County Championship in 2004.

A WRONG TURN

In March 1977 the Centenary Test was played between England and Australia at Melbourne to commemorate 100 years of Test cricket. England put Australia in to bat and they were all out for 138. Australia then dismissed England for 95. In their second innings Australia declared at 419 for 9, setting England a target of 463 runs for victory. Although England could not capitalize on their good start and eventually fell 45 runs short of the mark, at one point they were on 346 for 4, thanks to Derek Randall's outstanding 174. When Randall's innings ended, the 80,000 fans inside the Melbourne Cricket Ground gave him a standing ovation. Randall was so moved by the acclaim that he walked off the pitch with his head bowed and his bat in the air. He then proceeded to walk through the wrong gate and, when he eventually looked up, he found himself at the door to the Royal Box, where he was greeted by Prince Philip and not his captain.

Ⅲ

⌐ ASHES FEVER (12) ⌐

"The thing to remember is don't jump for joy."
Richie Benaud *advising England fans perched on rooftops around The Oval during the 2005 Ashes series*

⌐ WAS JACK THE RIPPER A CRICKETER? ⌐

Montague John Druitt was born on 15th August 1857 in Wimborne, Dorset. He was a fast bowler who played for Winchester College, Incogniti and Dorset, and was also a playing member of the MCC. On 4th December 1888 Druitt was found drowned in the Thames at Chiswick. It was believed that he took his own life. In 1894 Montague John Druitt was named as a suspect in the "Jack the Ripper" case by Sir Melville MacNaghten, the Chief Constable of London's CID, although there is insufficient evidence to substantiate this assertion. Indeed, some of Druitt's cricket commitments in 1888 have been cited in his defence, such as the match on 8th September, which began only eight hours after one of the Ripper's victims was found murdered.

⌐ INDIA NARROWLY AVOID FOLLOW-ON ⌐

At Lord's in 1990 India, with one wicket in hand, needed 24 runs to avoid the follow-on in the first Test of the three-match series. Kapil Dev played back the first two balls of the over and then hit Eddie Hemmings, England's off-spinner, for four consecutive sixes, thereby avoiding the follow-on. Off the next delivery, India's No. 11 batsman, Narendra Hirwani, was dismissed by Angus Fraser. This is the only instance in the history of cricket of a player hitting 24 runs in an over to avoid the follow-on. In their first innings, England produced some outstanding figures:

❖ Graham Gooch hit 333, then the sixth highest ever Test score (627 minutes, 485 balls, 3 sixes and 43 fours).
❖ The Graham Gooch/Allan Lamb partnership of 308 is the highest England partnership against India (276 minutes).
❖ England's score of 653–4 is their highest score against India.

In England's second innings, Gooch scored 123 (148 minutes, 113 balls, 13 fours and 4 sixes) for an aggregate score of 456, the highest ever in Tests and the second highest in first-class cricket. Meanwhile, Graham Gooch and Mike Atherton's partnership of 204 is the highest first-wicket partnership for England against India at Lord's.

III

~ GRAHAM GOOCH, OBE ~

Graham Alan Gooch was born in Whipps Cross Hospital, Leytonstone, in East London on 23rd July 1953. Gooch played first-class cricket from 1973 to 2000. In 1975, aged 21, the Essex batsman made his Test debut for England against Australia but ended up bagging a "pair". In the following game of the series, he fared slightly better, scoring 6 and 31, but this was not deemed good enough to keep him in the side. Three years elapsed before Gooch was selected again by England, and in 1979 he played a major part in helping Essex capture their first County Championship. In 1980 he was named as one of *Wisden*'s Cricketers of the Year but, two years later, Gooch courted controversy by leading the first England rebel tour of South Africa. He was subsequently banned from Test cricket for three years. In 1988 Graham was one of *Indian Cricket*'s Cricketers of the Year Award and was appointed England captain.

In 1990, Gooch scored a record 456 runs in the Lord's Test against India, notching up a remarkable 333 in the first innings followed by 123 in the second. This is the only occasion to date in first-class cricket where a batsman has scored a triple century and a century in the same match. At Headingley in 1991, Graham hit 154 not out against the West Indies to clinch victory for England against a ferocious West Indian bowling attack. Gooch carried his bat in the second innings while only two of his team-mates managed to record double figures.

During the early 1990s Graham Gooch was widely regarded as one of the leading batsmen in world cricket. After the fourth Test of the 1993 Ashes series his fellow opening batsman, Michael Atherton, was made the new England captain. In 1995, aged 42, Graham Gooch retired from Test match cricket as England's all-time highest run-scorer with 8,900 runs, including 20 centuries. In total, Gooch scored 44,841 runs in first-class cricket at an average of 49.01, with 128 centuries. In addition to his ability to wield a bat with tremendous power and accuracy, Gooch also bowled occasional medium pace, taking over 200 first-class wickets. When a match was dead, Graham liked to entertain the crowd and would sometimes impersonate other bowlers, mimicking their bowling style.

Graham Gooch gave much to Essex, helping the county to six County Championships. In 1991 he was awarded the OBE for his services to cricket. Graham captained England 34 times in Tests (W10, D12, L12) and also in the 1992 World Cup final, which England lost to Pakistan. He also played in two other World Cup finals, in 1979 and 1987. Today, Gooch remains England's leading Test run-maker.

⫸

⸺ WETHERALL YOUNG ALL-ROUNDER ⸺

The Cricket Society's Wetherall Award for the Leading Young All-Rounder in English first-class cricket was first awarded in 1994. It was not awarded in 1997, 2000, 2001 or 2003. The winners were:

1994	Adam Hollioake (Surrey)
1995	Richard Rollins (Essex)
1996	Ashley Giles (Warwickshire)
1998	Darren Thomas (Glamorgan)
1999	Graeme Swann (Northamptonshire)
2002	Graeme Swann (Northamptonshire)
2004	Jamie Dalrymple (Middlesex)
2005	Ravi Bopara (Essex)

⸺ GLADSTONE SMALL ⸺

Gladstone Cleophas Small was born in St George, Barbados, on 18 October 1961. Shortly after his 14th birthday, Small and his family moved to England. Undeterred by the normal rule at the time that a person could not change their nationality after their 14th birthday, Small applied for eligibility to play cricket for England, and the MCC accepted his application. Small was primarily an out-swing bowler and his early erratic bowling very often gave England's selectors a headache or two when it came to deciding whether or not to pick him. However, during the 1986/87 Ashes series, Small came into the side for the fourth Test as a last-minute replacement and lit up the match, taking 5 for 48 in Australia's first innings and then claiming two wickets in their second innings. His performance in the game won him the Man of the Match award. Gladstone was always a very committed team player and was a key member of the strong Warwickshire side of 1994, but retired soon after. In 2005, Small was appointed a Director of the Professional Cricketers' Association.

⸺ THE FIRST ONE-DAY INTERNATIONAL ⸺

Australia and England contested the first ever one-day international match at Melbourne in 1971. The match came about as a direct result of the weather. The first four days of the scheduled Test match between the two countries had been rained out, so on the final day a one-day international was organised. Australia won the 40-over match by five wickets.

II

⟶ MAGIC NUMBERS ⟶

Every individual score up to and including 227 has been recorded by a batsman in a Test match. However, no batsman has ever finished an innings on 228, and no one has recorded a score of 229 either. Walter Hammond and Vinod Kambli have both been out for 227, and Bert Sutcliffe of New Zealand once scored 230 not out. In first-class cricket a number of batsmen have recorded a score of 228, including Darren Bicknell, Ian Botham, Keith Fletcher, Archie MacLaren and Hanif Mohammad.

⟶ AN INDIAN CURRY FOR GOWER ⟶

When India unexpectedly won the 1983 Prudential World Cup, beating England in the semi-finals and the West Indies in the Final, the cricketing world was unimpressed and thought the Indians were mere one-tournament wonders. However, India proved the doubters wrong when they visited Australia in the 1985 Benson & Hedges World Cup. They played magnificently and put in some outstanding performances on their way to winning the tournament. When they played England at the Sydney Cricket Ground, an English fan on the famous Hill held aloft a banner that read: "GIVE 'EM CURRY, DAVID GOWER". England were chasing 225 runs to win, but the run-rate reached impossible levels as India's bowlers gave nothing away. Eventually, in the place on the scoreboard where the required run-rate for victory is normally displayed, just one word appeared: "PRAY". India won the match by 86 runs, whereupon a delighted Indian supporter unveiled his own banner that read: "DID THE PRESSURE COOKER BLOW UP IN YOUR FACE, DAVID GOWER?"

⟶ RUPEES FOR RUNS ⟶

When England's Denis Compton arrived in India to play for Holkar against Bombay in the Ranji Trophy final of 1944/45, he was approached by a wealthy Bombay merchant and promised 50 rupees for every run he made over a hundred. In his first innings Compton was out lbw for 20. When he returned to the dressing-room after his second innings with a score of 249 not out, a dismayed Compton found a note from the businessman saying: "Sorry, Mr Compton, I'm called away on very urgent business."[†]

[†] *At the time the Ranji Trophy final of 1944/45 was the highest-scoring match ever. Bombay won by 374 runs, scoring an aggregate of 1,266 to Holkar's 852.*

Ⅲ

∽ WORLD CUP FINALS (3) ∽

The 1992 Cricket World Cup was the fifth to be staged and, co-hosted by Australia and New Zealand, the first to be contested in the Southern hemisphere. It took place from 22 February to 25 March, and for the first time day/night matches were introduced, as well as white cricket balls and coloured team uniforms. South Africa participated for the first time after the lifting of their 22-year ban, making nine nations in all – the eight Test-playing countries of the time, plus Zimbabwe. For the third time, England reached the final, this time facing Pakistan. From 70 for 2 after 25 overs, Pakistan stepped on the gas and added 153 from the last 20 overs to set a target of 250 to win. As in 1987, the England reply began badly, Ian Botham out for a duck. Their one partnership of any subtance – 72 from Allan Lamb and Neil Fairbrother – was finally ended by Man of the Match Wasim Akram and England ended 22 runs adrift.

ENGLAND V PAKISTAN

25 MARCH 1992, MELBOURNE CRICKET GROUND, AUSTRALIA

Result: Pakistan won by 22 runs. Toss: Pakistan. *Umpires:* BL Aldridge, SA Bucknor

PAKISTAN			Runs	Mins	Balls	4s	6s
Aamer Sohail	c Stewart	b Pringle	4	20	19	0	0
Rameez Raja	lbw	b Pringle	8	36	26	1	0
*Imran Khan	c Illingworth	b Botham	72	159	110	5	1
Javed Miandad	c Botham	b Illingworth	58	125	98	4	0
Inzamam-ul-Haq		b Pringle	42	46	35	4	0
Wasim Akram	run out		33	21	19	4	0
Saleem Malik	not out		0	2	1	0	0
Extras	(lb 19, w 6, nb 7)		32				
TOTAL	(6 wickets, 50 overs)		249				

DidNot Bat: Ijaz Ahmed, +Moin Khan, Mushtaq Ahmed, Aaqib Javed.

FoW: 1/20 (Aamer Sohail), 2/24 (Rameez Raja), 3/163 (Javed Miandad), 4/197 (Imran Khan), 5/249 (Inzamam-ul-Haq), 6/249 (Wasim Akram).

Bowling	O	M	R	W
Pringle	10	2	22	3
Lewis	10	2	52	0
Botham	7	0	42	1
DeFreitas	10	1	42	0
Illingworth	10	0	50	1
Reeve	3	0	22	0

III

ENGLAND			Runs	Mins	Balls	4s	6s
*GA Gooch	c Aaqib	b Mushtaq	29	93	66	1	0
IT Botham	c Moin	b Wasim	0	12	6	0	0
†AJ Stewart	c Moin	b Aaqib	7	22	16	1	0
GA Hick	lbw	b Mushtaq	17	49	36	1	0
NH Fairbrother	c Moin	b Aaqib	62	97	70	3	0
AJ Lamb		b Wasim	31	54	41	2	0
CC Lewis		b Wasim	0	6	1	0	0
DA Reeve	c Rameez	b Mushtaq	15	38	32	0	0
DR Pringle	not out		18	29	16	1	0
PAJ DeFreitas	run out		10	13	8	0	0
RK Illingworth	c Rameez	b Imran	14	9	11	2	0
Extras	(lb 5, w 13, nb 6)		24				
TOTAL	(all out, 49.2 overs)		227				

FoW:1/6 (Botham), 2/21 (Stewart), 3/59 (Hick), 4/69 (Gooch), 5/141 (Lamb), 6/141 (Lewis), 7/180 (Fairbrother), 8/183 (Reeve), 9/208 (DeFreitas), 10/227 (Illingworth).

Bowling	O	M	R	W
Wasim Akram	10	0	49	3
Aaqib Javed	10	2	27	2
Mushtaq Ahmed	10	1	41	3
Ijaz Ahmed	3	0	13	0
Imran Khan	6.2	0	43	1
Aamer Sohail	10	0	49	0

Did You Know That?

Derek Pringle is the only England bowler to have taken three wickets in a World Cup final. He is also the only England bowler to have recorded an economy rate of less than 2.5 runs per over in a final.

⟿ BEDSER'S BRADMAN DOUBLE ⟾

On 3 February 1947, England's Alec Bedser bowled Don Bradman out for a duck in the first innings of the fourth Test of the series at the Adelaide Oval. A year later, at Trent Bridge on 15 June 1948, Bedser once again got Bradman for a duck, this time caught by Len Hutton. However, in his ten Test innings between those ducks, the Don scored 974 runs, with four centuries and a double-hundred.

⟿ A DOLPHIN PLAYS FOR ENGLAND ⟾

Arthur Dolphin played in one Test match for England in 1921.

III

⌐ FANTASY ENGLAND XI (13) ⌐

SOMERSET

1	*Marcus* TRESCOTHICK
2	*Mark* LATHWELL
3	*Harold* GIMBLETT
4	*Leonard* BRAUND
5	*Brian* ROSE *(CAPTAIN)*
6	*Ian* BOTHAM
7	*Sammy* WOODS
8	*Leslie* GAY *(WICKET-KEEPER)*
9	*Vic* MARKS
10	*Arthur* WELLARD
11	*Andy* CADDICK
12th Man	*Fred* RUMSEY

Did You Know That?

Somerset CCC joined the County Championship in 1891. In their second season, 1892, Somerset finished third, but it would be another 66 years before they reached such a high position again. They have an unwanted record, having finished bottom of the table a record 12 times (plus one shared wooden spoon). Somerset are one of only four counties never to have won the County Championship.

⌐ 5 NARROWEST TEST WINNING MARGINS ⌐

England appear three times at the top the table for Test victories by the smallest margins of runs:

Pos.	Margin	Teams	Venue	Year
1.	1 run	West Indies (252 & 146) beat Australia (213 & 184)	Adelaide	1992/93
2.	2 runs	England (407 & 182) beat Australia (308 & 279)	Birmingham	2005
=3.	3 runs	Australia (299 & 86) beat England (262 & 120)	Manchester	1902
=3.	3 runs	England (284 & 294) beat Australia (287 & 288)	Melbourne	1982/83
5.	5 runs	South Africa (169 & 239) beat Australia (292 & 111)	Sydney	1993/94

⟡ BARMY ARMY SONG (3) ⟡

Is This the Way to Win the Ashes?
(To the tune of "Is This the Way to Amarillo?")
When the day is dawning
On a sunny Thursday morning
How we long to be there
With the Army drinking a beer there
Every run and wicket, on every single day
We want to see the cricket, and the Ashes here to stay

Is this the way to win the Ashes
Vaughany strokes and Freddy smashes
Dreaming dreams of winning the Ashes
And sending convicts home again.
Show me the way to win the Ashes
Gilo's guile gets blades a-flashing
Thorpey bagging loads of catches
To send the convicts home again

Tresco and Straussy starting
Leaving McGrath and Dizzy smarting
Then the Brett Lee no-balls,
Bringing even more four balls
Then they bring on Warnie
He goes the distance too
Flying over Langer
But he's only five foot two...

Is this the way to win the Ashes
Vaughany strokes and Freddy smashes
Dreaming dreams of winning the Ashes
And sending convicts home again.
Show me the way to win the Ashes
Gilo's guile gets blades a-flashing
Thorpey bagging loads of catches
To send the convicts home again

Sha la la lala lalala...

Courtesy of Gary Taylor

Ⅲ

"In Affectionate Remembrance of English Cricket, which died at the Oval on 29th August 1882. Deeply lamented by a large circle of sorrowing friends and acquaintances. RIP. NB – The body will be cremated and the ashes taken to Australia."
Reginald Brooks – spoof obituary in the Sporting Times, *1882*

~ OUT "HANDLED THE BALL" ~

Five batsmen have been given out "handled the ball" in a Test match. South Africa's Russell Endean was the first victim against England in the second innings of the second Test at Cape Town in 1956/57. Next was Australia's Andrew Hilditch against Pakistan again in the second innings of the second Test at Perth in 1978/79, followed by Mohsin Khan of Pakistan against Australia in the first innings of the first Test at Karachi in 1982/83. Desmond Haynes of the West Indies went this way in the first innings of the fourth Test against India in Bombay in 1983/84. England's Graham Gooch handled the ball in the second innings of the opening Test against Australia at Old Trafford in 1993.

~ ORIGIN OF THE TERM "BODYLINE" ~

In 1932, Hugh Buggy, a journalist from Sydney working for the *Sydney Sun*, sent a telegram to his newspaper following a day's play in the Australia v England Ashes Test in Sydney. As the telegram company charged for the number of words used, he replaced "in the line of the body" with the term "bodyline" to keep down the cost of the telegram.

~ BRILLIANT BOSIE ~

In addition to cricket, Bernard Bosanquet, who invented the googly or Bosie as it was known at the time in his honour, represented Oxford University at billiards in 1898 and 1900 and at hammer throwing in 1899 and 1900.

~ ABEL'S VERY ABLE ~

The Surrey and England opening batsman, Robert "Bobby" Abel, was the first England player to "carry his bat" through a Test innings, scoring 132 not out against Australia in 1892.

III

⌒ BAD AWAY DAYS (3) ⌒

South Africa's tour of England, 1970

This was deemed "the tour that never was". Prior to England's tour of South Africa in 1968/69, the South African government took exception to the inclusion in the touring party of Basil D'Oliveira, a non-white who had emigrated from the Cape to play in England. B.J. Vorster, the prime minister of South Africa, said D'Oliveira was unacceptable as a member of the MCC side, and the tour was cancelled. In 1970, a "Stop the Tour" campaign prevented South Africa touring England.

⌒ ENGLAND'S GREATEST POST-WAR XI ⌒

In October 2004, *The Wisden Cricketer* magazine published England's Greatest Post-War XI. This team of post-war champions was selected by a panel made up of Rajan Bala, Alex Bannister, Jack Bannister, Sir Alec Bedser, Scyld Berry, Dickie Bird, Geoff Boycott, Mike Denness, Matthew Engel, David Frith, Tom Graveney, Tony Greig, Walter Hadlee, Ray Illingworth, Doug Insole, Tony Lewis, Steven Lynch, Christopher Martin-Jenkins, Graeme Pollock, Bob Simpson, Micky Stewart, Sir Clyde Walcott, Simon Wilde, Bob Willis and John Woodcock. The 25-man panel were given the task of picking a balanced side to compete in a five-day Test with a premium placed on attractive, attacking cricket. The following side was chosen and is listed in batting order:

1. Len Hutton, captain (Yorkshire)
2. Graham Gooch (Essex)
3. Peter May (Surrey)
4. Denis Compton (Middlesex)
5. Ken Barrington (Surrey)
6. Ian Botham (Somerset, Worcestershire and Durham)
7. Alan Knott (Kent) *wicketkeeper*
8. Jim Laker (Surrey)
9. Fred Trueman (Yorkshire)
10. Alec Bedser (Surrey)
11. Derek Underwood (Kent)

⌒ SENSATIONAL ENGLAND COLLAPSE ⌒

During a one-day international against India at Gwalior on 4th March 1993, England lost their last 7 wickets for a mere 10 runs!

DR W.G. GRACE

W.G. Grace was born on 18 July 1848 in North Street, Downend, near Bristol. In 1865, aged 16, he started playing cricket for Gloucestershire and after 44 seasons, in 1908 – well into his 60th year – he played his final first-class match. In 1871 he scored a mammoth 2,739 runs in a season, and in 1876 he scored 344 for the MCC v Kent at Canterbury. William Gilbert Grace became Dr W.G. Grace in 1879, after passing his medical degree, and opened a practice in Bristol. His greatest honour came in 1880 when, on his Test debut, he captained England against Australia at The Oval. Opening with his brother, he scored 152 in the first innings of England's impressive five-wicket victory.

For many years Grace played for Gloucestershire and saw the county crowned champions three times and joint champions once between 1873 and 1877. W.G. scored 54,896 runs – average 39.55 – still the fifth highest aggregate of all time. Grace was equally dangerous as a bowler, taking 2,876 wickets – average 17.92 – the sixth highest total ever. He completed a double of 2,000 runs and 100 wickets in a season in both 1873 and 1876. He also took a staggering 887 catches, which remains the second highest number of catches taken by anyone in their career.

Despite his huge frame, W.G. was a player of tremendous stamina and agility. In addition to his outstanding cricketing abilities, Grace was also a keen player of bowls and golf. A disciplinarian, he took no nonsense from his players and if any of them turned up late he would put them in to bat last. Grace revolutionized the game of cricket by encouraging, among other things, competition among the players and the teams, swing bowling, and shots being played off the back foot.

Although W.G. Grace played Test cricket for England from 1880 to 1899 he only played in 22 Tests, but series usually comprised only two or three matches. He captained England in five Ashes series, one of which was in Australia. In 1908 he retired from first-class cricket but continued to play in other games. On 25 July 1914, aged 66, he played his last game and in typical style he scored 69 not out. When he died in October 1915, the news of his death shook the nation.

He was named *Wisden*'s Cricketer of the Year in 1896, the first of only four occasions when the award was not shared.

Did You Know That?

W.G.'s brother, E.M. Grace, was a coroner, and he once arranged to have a corpse placed on a bed of ice so that he could examine it after the cricket match in which he was playing had finished.

III

◦ YOUNGEST / OLDEST TEST HAT-TRICKS ◦

The youngest player to take a Test hat-trick is Bangladesh's fast bowler Alok Kapali, aged 19 years and 240 days; the oldest player is the England off-spinner, Tom Goddard, aged 38 years and 87 days.

◦ SIR NEVILLE CARDUS ◦

Sir Neville Cardus is regarded as the best cricket writer of all time. His description of the matches that he covered was so vivid and colourful that all cricket writers that followed him have been judged on his reporting brilliance.

Always conscious of the finer points of style, when Sir Neville was on a tour he used to cable words like "comma" and "semi-colon" to show how his report should be punctuated. In the mid-1900s, telegraph companies charged for every word in a cabled message, and as a result of his emphasis on punctuation in his messages, his cabled reports cost a lot of money to send. One newspaper editor, concerned about the expense of Sir Neville's cables, sent him a return cable saying: "Please send story. We'll fix punctuation." Sir Neville swiftly replied: "I'll send punctuation. You fill in words."

◦ ALAN, GEOFF AND IAN ◦

The third Test at Trent Bridge in the 1977 Ashes series saw Geoff Boycott return to the England side after a three-year self-imposed exile (he scored 107 & 80 not out). The match also marked Ian Botham's Test debut (he took 5 for 74), while Alan Knott became the first wicket-keeper to pass 4,000 runs in Tests.

◦ LAKER ENRAGES THE AUTHORITIES ◦

In 1960 Jim Laker published a book entitled *Over to Me* which enraged the authorities at Lord's and The Oval so much that they withdrew his honorary memberships of MCC and Surrey respectively. However, both these positions were later restored, and at the time of his death Jim Laker was chairman of Surrey's cricket committee.

◦ BOWLED OUT ON THE SAME DAY ◦

In 1952 England dismissed India at Old Trafford twice on the same day for scores of just 58 and 82. It was the first time in Test match history that a team had been bowled out twice on the same day.

III

◦ ONE DOOR CLOSES, ANOTHER OPENS ◦

The legendary W.G. Grace played in his last ever Test match for England at Trent Bridge in the first Test of the 1899 Ashes series. A future England legend, Wilfred Rhodes, made his England Test debut in the same match.

◦ KING OF THE JUNGLE ◦

In 2002 eight celebrities were thrown into the Australian outback to compete head-to-head in the second series of the ITV show *I'm a Celebrity, Get Me Out of Here!* to determine who would be crowned "King/Queen of the Jungle". Viewers got to vote on who would participate in bush tucker trials, a food competition to see if the contestant could earn more food than the basic rations set for them in a day. But ultimately the viewers just voted for their favourite celebrity – whoever they wanted to win the title. After two weeks of trials and tribulations, England cricketer Phil Tufnell emerged from the Australian outback as the "King of the Jungle". John Fashanu, a former professional footballer, came second, and BBC television's *Changing Rooms* decorator Linda Barker came third.

◦ CAPTAIN BEEFY ◦

Ian Botham captained England 12 times between 1980 and 1981. Although he was not a successful captain, with eight draws and four losses, it should be said in his defence that nine of England's matches during his captaincy were against the best team in the world at the time, the West Indies.

◦ CAUGHT OUT ◦

During the late 1980s it was claimed that Ian Botham had a fling with a Barbados beauty queen that ended up with a broken bed in a hotel room. In the early 1990s Ian Botham released a book entitled *Don't Tell Kath*.

◦ AMISS THE FIRST ODI CENTURY MAKER ◦

England opening batsman Dennis Amiss was the first man to score a century in the one-day international. He reached 103, from 134 balls (nine fours), against Australia at Old Trafford on 24 August 1972. England made 226 for 4 and beat Australia (222) by six wickets

III

⟶ ENGLAND'S TOP TEST RUN-MAKERS ⟵

Batsman	M	I	NO	Runs	HS	Ave.	100	50	0	90
GA Gooch	118	215	6	8,900	333	42.58	20	46	13	3
AJ Stewart	133	235	21	8,463	190	39.55	15	45	14	2
DI Gower	117	204	18	8,231	215	44.25	18	39	7	2
G Boycott	108	193	23	8,114	246*	47.73	22	42	10	6
MA Atherton	115	212	7	7,728	185*	37.70	16	46	20	5
MC Cowdrey	114	188	15	7,624	182	44.07	22	38	9	4
WR Hammond	85	140	16	7,249	336*	58.46	22	24	4	1
L Hutton	79	138	15	6,971	364	56.67	19	33	5	3
KF Barrington	82	131	15	6,806	256	58.67	20	35	5	5
GP Thorpe	100	179	28	6,744	200*	44.66	16	39	12	2
DCS Compton	78	131	15	5,807	278	50.06	17	28	10	3
N Hussain	96	171	16	5,764	207	37.19	14	33	14	2
ME Trescothick	69	131	10	5,502	219	45.47	13	28	11	2
JB Hobbs	61	102	7	5,410	211	56.95	15	28	4	3
IT Botham	102	161	6	5,200	208	33.55	14	22	14	-
JH Edrich	77	127	9	5,138	310*	43.54	12	24	6	3
TW Graveney	79	123	13	4,882	258	44.38	11	20	8	4
AJ Lamb	79	139	10	4,656	142	36.09	14	18	9	2
MP Vaughan	64	115	8	4,595	197	42.94	15	14	7	-
H Sutcliffe	54	84	9	4,555	194	60.73	16	23	2	2

*Up to and including the Test series v Pakistan in November 2005

⟶ OKEY'S RECORD BEATEN ⟵

A.E. Osche, nicknamed "Okey" by his team-mates, set a South African cricket record which stood for more than one hundred years when he became the country's youngest Test cricketer. He took the field for the first Test against England at St George's Park, Port Elizabeth, on 12th March 1889, aged just 19 years and one day. It was South Africa's first ever Test match. His record was only beaten in December 1995 when Paul Adams, aged 18 years and 340 days, played against England in Port Elizabeth.

⟶ A CRAZY RUN-OUT ⟵

During England's one-day international match against Pakistan in Perth in January 1987, Rameez Raja was caught off a no-ball but, failing to hear the umpire's call, he left his crease to return to the pavilion thinking he was out. The bails were then removed and he was given "run out" by the square-leg umpire.

III

⌐ DICKY EXHAUSTED ⌐

England's Dicky Bird umpired in a one-day international Champions Trophy series at Sharjah in 1988. Sadly, he became so dehydrated while standing in a match between Pakistan and the West Indies that he had to retire to the cool sanctuary of the umpires' room.

⌐ BAD AWAY DAYS (4) ⌐

England's tour of Pakistan, 1987

The second Test in Faisalabad was soured by an unsavoury incident involving the England captain, Mike Gatting, and umpire Shakoor Rana. The incident occurred in the last over of the second day, with Pakistan struggling on 106 for 5 in reply to England's first-innings 292. Hemmings bowled his fourth delivery and the umpire, Khizar Hayat, called a "dead ball" as Gatting seemingly had moved a fielder without the batsman's knowledge. Rana, standing at square leg, stopped the game and warned Gatting about "unfair play". An angry Gatting stood waving his finger and arguing with the bewildered Rana, insults and bad language filling the air. Rana refused to umpire the match on the third day, demanding an apology from Gatting, who he claimed had called him a "cheat". Gatting was not to be moved, and a day's play was lost as Gatting and Rana each waited for the other to apologise. The TCCB eventually insisted on Gatting writing an apology so that play could be resumed on the fourth day. England then bowled Pakistan out for 191, but had lost the opportunity of levelling the series before the final Test in Karachi. England's second-innings declaration on 137 for 6 left no time for Pakistan to chase the runs, so play was called off and the match declared a draw. As a result of the Gatting-Rana affair the England team were paid £1,000 each as a "hardship bonus".

⌐ ASHES FEVER (14) ⌐

"There are two teams out there. One of them is attempting to play cricket and the other is not."
Bill Woodfull, *Australian captain, gives his verdict on the Third Test at Adelaide in 1932/33*

⌐ THE GRAND OLD MAN OF CRICKET ⌐

The oldest Test captain was the legendary W.G. Grace, aged 50 years 320 days, in 1899.

Ⅲ

⌁ FANTASY ENGLAND XI (14) ⌁

                                    SURREY

1	*Jack* HOBBS
2	*John* EDRICH
3	*Peter* MAY *(CAPTAIN)*
4	*Graham* THORPE
5	*Ken* BARRINGTON
6	*Alec* STEWART
7	*Herbert* STRUDWICK *(WICKET-KEEPER)*
8	*Tony* LOCK
9	*Jim* LAKER
10	*Alec* BEDSER
11	*Geoff* ARNOLD
12th Man	*Adam* HOLLIOAKE

Did You Know That?
Surrey CCC is based at The Oval, London. Surrey won the inaugural County Championship in 1890 and between 1887 and 1895, they won eight County titles. Surrey also won seven consecutive championships from 1952 to 1958 and a total of 22 overall. The club badge is the Prince of Wales's three feathers which Lord Rosebery got permission to use from the Prince of Wales himself in 1915 as he owned the land on which The Oval was built.

⌁ UNUSUAL BOWLING FIGURES ⌁

During England's second Test against New Zealand at Trent Bridge in 1986, David Gower's bowling figures were highly unusual: 0.0–0–4–0. When Gower came on to bowl, his first delivery was called a no-ball, the umpire ruling that Gower's arm was suspiciously bent. However, Martin Crowe hit the delivery for four, which won the game, so Gower did not have to bowl again.

⌁ POSH GAME ⌁

In 1629, Henry Cuffen, the curate of Ruckinge, near Romney Marsh in Kent, was censured by the Church when after evening prayers he went and "played crickets". Cuffen defended himself on the grounds that cricket was played by people of quality.

England, under skipper Michael Vaughan, went into the fifth Test of the 2003 home series against South Africa trailing 2–1. The match, at The Oval, began on 4 September. South Africa captain Graeme Smith called correctly at the toss and elected to bat.

At the end of a glorious first day's play South Africa lost two late wickets, but still finished on 362 for 4, with Herschelle Gibbs making 183 and Gary Kirsten 90, both batsmen falling to Ashley Giles. The next day South Africa added a further 122 runs, advancing to 484 all out, with Jacques Kallis being run out for 66. Martin Bicknell, 2 for 71, Giles, 2 for 102, and Jimmy Anderson, 2 for 86, led the wicket-takers, but the South Africans did suffer three run-outs.

Marcus Trescothick and Michael Vaughan set off in pursuit of South Africa's first innings score, and by the close on the second day England had made 165 for 2, with Trescothick and Graham Thorpe unbeaten on 64 and 28, respectively. Vaughan had gone for 23 and Mark Butcher had fallen for 32. England batted with calm assurance on the third day and ended it with a lead of 18 on 502 for 7. The day had belonged to Trescothick, who accounted for 219 of England's impressive tally, and to Thorpe, who made 124 on his Test comeback.

Andrew Flintoff took centre stage on day four. Starting 10 not out, he lost Bicknell for a duck to the third ball of the day. Steve Harmison was an almost silent partner (he scored three) as Flintoff smashed 85 off 77 balls (11 fours, 4 sixes) in a 99-run partnership. Flintoff was bowled by Paul Adams for 95 and England declared three runs later, on 604 for 9, a lead of 120. South Africa struggled in their second innings, reaching 185 for 6 at the close of play.

Bicknell and Harmison were clinical, finishing with four wickets each as South Africa added just 44 to end up 229 all out. England had a target of just 110 to claim an improbable victory, especially after South Africa had been 345 for 2. Bookmakers had offered odds of 40/1 against an England victory before their first innings. England went at almost five runs per over as they achieved the target with 9 wickets in hand, Trescothick adding 69 not out to his 219.

Did You Know That?

This was only the seventh occasion in Test history that a team had conceded 450 runs or more in the first innings of a match and still won. Australia had managed two wins, India one, and South Africa one. England had done this twice, too, in 1894/95 Australia (586 & 166) lost to England (325 & 437) and in 1967/68 the West Indies (526–7 & 92–2) lost to England (404 & 215–3).

ENGLAND V SOUTH AFRICA – Fifth Test

4–8 SEPTEMBER 2003, THE OVAL, LONDON

Result: England won by 9 wickets. *Toss:* South Africa. *Umpires:* SJA Taufel, S Venkataraghavan.

SOUTH AFRICA

*GC Smith	run out (Vaughan)		18	lbw	b Bicknell	19
HH Gibbs		b Giles	183	c Stewart	b Anderson	9
G Kirsten	lbw	b Giles	90	c Trescothick	b Harmison	29
JH Kallis	run out (Giles)		66	lbw	b Harmison	35
ND McKenzie	c Stewart	b Anderson	9	lbw	b Flintoff	38
JA Rudolph	lbw	b Bicknell	0		b Bicknell	8
†MV Boucher	c Stewart	b Bicknell	8	c Stewart	b Bicknell	25
SM Pollock	not out		66	c Thorpe	b Harmison	43
AJ Hall	lbw	b Flintoff	1	c Smith	b Bicknell	0
PR Adams	run out (Butcher/Giles)		1	not out		13
M Ntini		b Anderson	11	c Smith	b Harmison	1
Extras	(b 12, lb 10, w 4, nb 5)		31	(b 1, lb 7, nb 1)		9
TOTAL	(all out)		484	(all out)		229

1/63, 2/290, 3/345, 4/362, 5/365
6/385, 7/419, 8/421, 9/432, 10/484

1/24, 2/34, 3/92, 4/93, 5/118
6/150, 7/193, 8/193, 9/215, 10/229

Bowling: *First Innings:* Bicknell 20–3–71–2, Anderson 25–6–86–2, Harmison 27–8–73–0, Giles 29–3–102–2, Flintoff 19–4–88–1, Vaughan 5–0–24–0, Butcher 3–0–18–0. *Second Innings:* Bicknell 24–5–84–4, Anderson 10–1–55–1, Harmison 19.2–8–33–4, Giles 10–2–36–0, Flintoff 6–2–13–1.

ENGLAND

ME Trescothick	c Rudolph	b Ntini	219	not out		69
*MP Vaughan	c Gibbs	b Pollock	23	c Boucher	b Kallis	13
MA Butcher	lbw	b Hall	32	not out		20
GP Thorpe		b Kallis	124			
ET Smith	lbw	b Hall	16			
†AJ Stewart	lbw	b Pollock	38			
A Flintoff		b Adams	95			
AF Giles	c Hall	b Kallis	2			
MP Bicknell	lbw	b Pollock	0			
SJ Harmison	not out		6			
JM Anderson	not out		0			
Extras	(b 11, lb 18, w 9, nb 11)		49	(lb 4, nb 4)		8
TOTAL	(for 9 wickets declared)		604	(for 1 wicket)		110

1/28, 2/78, 3/346, 4/379, 5/480
6/489, 7/502, 8/502, 9-601

1/47

Bowling: *First Innings:* Pollock 39–10–111–3, Ntini 31–4–129–1, Hall 35–5–111–2, Kallis 34–5–117–2, Adams 17–2–79–1, Rudolph 6–1–28–0. *Second Innings:* Pollock 6–0–15–0, Ntini 8–0–46–0, Kallis 5.2–0–25–1, Adams 3–0–20–0.

FIRST TEST TON FOR BANNERMAN

The first century in Test cricket was scored by Australia's Charlie Bannerman[†] during the inaugural Test between England and Australia in 1877.

STRAUSS JOINS ELITE CLUB

Andrew Strauss scored 112 in his first innings for England against New Zealand at Lord's in May 2004 to become the fifteenth England batsman to record a century on his Test debut and the fourth batsman overall to do so at Lord's after Henry Graham for Australia in 1893, John Hampshire for England in 1969 and Sourav Ganguly for India in 1996. Before Strauss, Graham Thorpe was the last England batsman to score a century on Test debut when he hit 114 not out against Australia in 1993.

WILLIS HIT FOR 6 FOURS

Sandeep Patil of India was the first batsman in the world to hit six fours in an over in a Test match. He achieved this against England's Bob Willis at Old Trafford in 1982, but one boundary came off a no ball.

ENGLAND PLAYS IRANI

Ronnie Irani of Essex played for England in three Tests between 1996 and 1999 and in 31 one-day internationals between 1996 and 2002/03.

MOST ECONOMICAL TEST ANALYSIS

The most economical bowling performance by a bowler taking 10 or more wickets in a Test match was recorded by England's Johnny Briggs. In 1888/89, Briggs took 15 wickets for 28 runs against South Africa in Cape Town.

ENGLAND CAPTAIN'S DOUBLE BLUE

Former England captain Mike (M.J.K) Smith was a double Blue (cricket and rugby) during his time at Oxford University.

[†]*Although he played for Australia, Bannerman was born in Woolwich, Kent, on 3 July 1851.*

◦ SMITH SETS UNWANTED RECORD ◦

England's Robin Smith holds the record of having made the highest score in an ODI for the losing side. Smith scored 167 in a 55-over match against Australia at Birmingham on 21 May 1993.

◦ A LONG SPELL OF BOWLING ◦

Derek Shackleton made his England Test debut at Trent Bridge against the West Indies in July 1950 and 13 years later he played his last Test match, also against the men from the Caribbean. In 1962, Shackleton became the last bowler to bowl 10,000 balls in a season and was the leading first-class wicket-taker in England every year from 1962 to 1965.

◦ 50, 100 AND 5 WICKETS ◦

Ian Botham and Jacques Kallis (South Africa) are the only players who have scored a half-century, a century and taken five wickets in the same Test. Botham did it against Australia at Headingley in 1981; Kallis did it against the West Indies in Cape Town in 1999.

◦ OVER AND OUT ◦

The first and last man to hit a ball clean over the pavilion at Lord's was Albert Trott in 1899.

◦ JUST CALL ME "SIR" ◦

The first cricketer to be knighted was Sir Pelham Warner of Middlesex and England. The first cricket writer to be knighted was Sir Neville Cardus. Sir Neville once described the legendary Donald Bradman as "a genius with an eye for business".

◦ ROCKET BALL ◦

During the first Prudential Trophy one-day international match between England and the West Indies at North Marine Road, Scarborough, on 26 August 1976, Michael Holding threw a ball in from the boundary with such force that after hitting one set of stumps it went on to hit the other set. Despite both batsmen being out of their creases the umpire was too confused to give either one of them out.

▓

⌐ A MAN FOR ALL POSITIONS ⌐

Wilfred Rhodes of England was the first cricketer to bat at all 11 positions in Test cricket. Rhodes's feat was subsequently equalled by Mulvantrai "Vinoo" Mankad of India.

⌐ FASTEST CENTURY IN TEST CRICKET ⌐

The great West Indian Sir Vivian Richards holds the record for the fastest century in Test cricket in terms of balls faced. He reached his century off just 56 balls against England at St John's in 1985/86.

⌐ KING FOR A DAY ⌐

When England faced the West Indies at Lord's in the 1979 World Cup Final the West Indian all-rounder Collis King played an unforgettable innings. The West Indies were in trouble at 99 for 4 when he walked out to join Viv Richards. The crowd then watched in total amazement as King scored 86 from 66 balls, smashing everything England's bowlers tossed his way, and added 139 with Richards in just 21 overs. Their partnership put the match beyond England's reach.

⌐ FASTEST TEST DOUBLE CENTURY ⌐

Australia's legendary Don Bradman scored the fastest Test double-century, in terms of time at the crease, 214 minutes, during his innings of 334 against England at Headingley in 1930.[†]

⌐ NEW NINTH-WICKET ODI RECORD ⌐

In the second one-day international against Pakistan in the Gaddafi Stadium, Lahore, in December 2005, Liam Plunkett and Vikram Solanki compiled a record-breaking ninth-wicket partnership for England. Their 100 runs off 100 balls surpassed the previous best in a limited overs international, set when Andrew Flintoff and Andy Caddick notched up 55 against India in Durban in 2002/03. Despite Marcus Trescothick winning his second consecutive toss, England lost in Lahore after Shoaib Akhtar, the Man of the Match, claimed 5 wickets for only 54 runs.

[†]*Ian Botham hit a double century in 220 balls during his innings of 208 against India at the Oval in 1982*

▥

⟿ SIR JACK HOBBS ⟿

John Berry "Jack" Hobbs was born on 16 December 1882 in Cambridge. He was the eldest of 12 children, six boys and six girls, whose father was on the staff at Fenner's and stood as a professional umpire. During the school holidays Jack used to go to the nets and play his own version of cricket with the servants at Jesus College, where his father also worked as a groundsman. The young Hobbs improvised, using a tennis ball, a cricket stump for a bat and a tennis post for a wicket on a gravel pitch. At the age of 12, Jack joined his first cricket team, the Church Choir Eleven at St Matthew's, Cambridge, where he was a member of the choir, but his first innings was for the choir of Jesus College.

Jack's boyhood hero was Surrey's outstanding batsman Tom Hayward, and it was Hayward who was instrumental in Jack joining Surrey. Shortly after the death of Jack's father in 1902, Hayward arranged a benefit match for Jack's mother, and a close friend of the family asked Hayward to take a good look at Jack in the match. The young Hobbs batted for 20 minutes against William Reeves, the Essex bowler, and Hayward was so impressed with his batting that he promised Jack that he would get him a trial at The Oval the following spring. In April 1903 Hobbs joined Surrey, where he began his illustrious career with a duck when opening the batting for the Surrey Colts against Battersea at The Oval.

On 24 April 1905 Hobbs played his first first-class match for Surrey. The opponents were The Gentlemen of England, captained by the legendary W.G. Grace. The 22-year-old Hobbs scored 18 and 88, and after the game W.G. said that Hobbs was destined to be an excellent cricketer. Twenty years later Hobbs beat Grace's own career record of 126 centuries. Hobbs was nicknamed "The Master" and scored consistently throughout a long career that didn't end until he was in his fifties. Almost half (98) of his 197 centuries came when he was over 40, and to this day he remains the oldest man to score a Test century (aged 46 in 1928/29). In 1926, aged 44, he was named the *Wisden* Cricketer of the Year – the last of only four occasions when a single cricketer received the award.

Always the consummate cricketer, Hobbs scored more first-class runs in his career (61,237 – at an average of 50.65) and more first-class centuries than any other player. It is highly unlikely that these two records will ever be beaten as modern-day cricketers play fewer first-class matches. He also scored over 1,000 runs in a season no fewer than 26 times and scored a hundred before lunch 20 times. In 1953 he became the first professional cricketer to be knighted.

⫿

⌁ FANTASY ENGLAND XI (15) ⌁

SUSSEX

1................................*Alan* OAKMAN
2................*Rt Rev David* SHEPPARD
3.............................*Ted* DEXTER
4................*Kumar* RANJITSINHJI
5..............*Charles (C.B.)* FRY *(CAPTAIN)*
6.............................*Jim* PARKS *(WICKET-KEEPER)*
7............................*Tony* GREIG
8..........................*Ian* SALISBURY
9........................*Maurice* TATE
10.....................*C. Aubrey* SMITH
11...........................*John* SNOW
12th Man...*Kumar* DULEEPSINHJI

Did You Know That?

Sussex CCC is England's oldest County Cricket club in continuous existence, having been formed in 1839. Remarkably it had to wait 164 years to win its first, and to date, only County Championship title (2003). However, before the current County Championship officially began in 1890, an unofficial championship existed which Sussex won outright seven times between 1825 and 1889, and also shared it with Nottinghamshire in 1852.

⌁ ENGLAND'S FIRST CAPTAIN ⌁

England's first ever captain was James Lillywhite, Jr., who led the side in the inaugural Test of 1876/77. Lillywhite came from a family steeped in cricket tradition as five of his relations had all played for Sussex, whilst Lillywhite himself appeared in all of Sussex's matches from 1862 to 1881. He also holds the notable distinction of being the first Test player to officiate as an umpire in a Test match. Jim Lillywhite was the last survivor of the inaugural Test match and outlived the rest of his team-mates by seven years.

⌁ ENGLAND'S ZIMBABWEAN HICCUP ⌁

During the 1992 World Cup, Zimbabwe was the only team that England lost to en route to the final.

Ⅲ

⟿ BAD AWAY DAYS (5) ⟿

The England rebel tour of South Africa, 1989/90

In response to a worldwide sports boycott of the country as a result of its apartheid policies, South Africa staged a number of rebel cricket tours during the 1980s. Unbelievably, even non-white teams from Sri Lanka and the West Indies participated, but the one tour that stirred up more anger than any other was that of the England "rebel" side, captained by Mike Gatting. All of the England games were the target of threats, some protesters even claiming that they were prepared to commit murder on any field the team played on. Gatting himself was heavily criticized, and then the news of Nelson Mandela's imminent release from prison resulted in the curtailment of the tour.

⟿ ASHES FEVER (15) ⟿

"All Australians are an uneducated and unruly mob."
Douglas Jardine, *England captain, exercises his diplomatic skills in 1932–33*

⟿ ANDERSON'S PAKISTAN HAT-TRICK ⟿

James Anderson took 4 for 48 in the one-day international against Pakistan at Rawalpindi Stadium on 21 December 2005. It was the fifth time that he had taken 4 wickets or more in an ODI and the third time against Pakistan.

⟿ ODI MILESTONE FOR FLINTOFF ⟿

When Andrew Flintoff took 3 for 73 in the one-day international against Pakistan at Gaddafi Stadium, Lahore, on 8 December 2005, it took his aggregate to 100 ODI wickets, making him the fourth England player to achieve that milestone.

⟿ ONE HUNDRED CENTURIES ⟿

In 1894, both W.G. Grace and his county Gloucestershire had a disappointing season. Grace, who was 46, could only average 18 runs with the bat, and many at the time believed that for English cricket it was the end of an era. However, 12 months later, he recorded his hundredth century and passed 1,000 runs in May (averaging 51). In total he made 126 first-class hundreds.

Ⅲ

⤳ THE GREAT TEST MATCHES (11) ⤳

Despite having lost the toss, on 14 March 2004 England beat the West Indies by 10 wickets at Sabina Park, Kingston, Jamaica, in a remarkable first Test of their 2003/04 Caribbean tour.

The West Indies decided to bat first and reached the close on the first day on 311 for 9 (Corey Collymore, 3,and Fidel Edwards, 1, the not out batsmen). They were indebted to opener Devon Smith, with 108, and Roland Hinds, who contributed 84, because the other seven batsmen mustered just 98 between them. Early on the following morning the West Indies were all out for 311, failing to add to their overnight score. England lost both openers, Marcus Trescothick and captain Michael Vaughan, cheaply, but Mark Butcher and Nasser Hussain added 119 for the third wicket before Burtcher became Edwards' third victim of the innings. By stumps on day two, England were 154 for 3 (Hussain on 41 and Graham Thorpe 1).

A weather-affected third day saw England add a further 185 runs to their score, finally being bowled out for 339 a lead of 28. Strangely, the innings' top-scorer was Extras with 60 (7 byes, 28 leg byes, 7 wides and 18 no balls), followed by Nasser Hussain and Mark Butcher with 58 each. The West Indies finished the third day on 8 for 0 (Chris Gayle 8, Devon Smith 0).

When play resumed on the fourth day, Steve Harmison simply blew the West Indies away. They slumped from 13 for 0 to 21 for 5 as the Durham fast bowler, ably assisted by Matthew Hoggard, ripped out of the heart of the order, Ramnaresh Sarwan, Shivnarine Chanderpaul and captain Brian Lara all falling for ducks. Hinds and wicket-keeper Ridley Jacobs added 20 for the sixth wicket, but once Jacobs edged Harmison to Hussain, the writing was on the wall. The last five wickets fell for six runs as Harmison finished with figures of 7 for 12 (including his 50th Test wicket – Edwards caught by Trescothick) from 12.3 overs. The complete innings of 47 lasted just 25.3 overs, so England had a target of 20 runs to claim victory and Vaughan (11) and Trescothick (6) needed just 17 balls to take a 1–0 series lead.

Did You Know That?

Steve Harmison's 7 for 12 is the best ever bowling return at Sabina Park, whilst the West Indies' 47 all out in their second innings is their lowest ever completed Test innings, beating the previous low point of 51 versus Australia in the first Test of the 1998/99 series at Port of Spain, Trinidad. Harmison was one of *Wisden*'s Cricketers of the Year in 2005, and was awarded the MBE in the 2006 New Year Honours for his part in England's memorable 2005 Ashes victory.

WEST INDIES V ENGLAND – FIRST TEST

11–14 MARCH 2004, SABINA PARK, KINGSTON, JAMAICA

Result: England won by 10 wickets. *Toss:* West Indies. Umpires: BF Bowden, DJ Harper.

WEST INDIES

CH Gayle		b Harmison	5	c Thorpe	b Harmison	9
DS Smith	st Read	b Giles	108	c and b	Hoggard	12
RR Sarwan	lbw	b Hoggard	0	lbw	b Harmison	0
*BC Lara	c Flintoff	b Jones	23	(5) c Flintoff	b Hoggard	0
S Chanderpaul		b Hoggard	7	(4)	b Harmison	0
RO Hinds	c Butcher	b Giles	84	c Read	b Jones	3
†RD Jacobs	c Vaughan	b Jones	38	c Hussain	b Harmison	15
TL Best	lbw	b Harmison	20	c Read	b Harmison	0
A Sanford	c Trescothick	b Flintoff	1	c Trescothick	b Harmison	1
CD Collymore	not out		3	not out		2
FH Edwards	c Flintoff	b Hoggard	1		b Harmison	0
Extras	(lb 6, w 1, nb 14)		21	(lb 4, nb 1)		5
TOTAL	(all out)		311	(all out)		47

1/17, 2/22, 3/73, 4/101, 5/223
6/281, 7/289, 8/300, 9/307, 10/313

1/13, 2/13, 3/15, 4/16, 5/21
6/41, 7/41, 8/43, 9/43, 10/47

Bowling: *First Innings:* Hoggard 18.4–3–68–3, Harmison 21–6–61–2, Flintoff 16–3–45–1, Jones 18–2–62–2, Giles 12–0–67–2, Vaughan 1–0–2–0. *Second Innings:* Hoggard 9–2–21–2, Harmison 12.3–8–12–7, Jones 4–1–10–1.

ENGLAND

ME Trescothick		b Edwards	7	not out	6
*MP Vaughan	c Lara	b Edwards	15	not out	11
MA Butcher	c Jacobs	b Edwards	58		
N Hussain	c sub (Bernard)	b Best	58		
GP Thorpe	c Sanford	b Best	19		
A Flintoff	c Hinds	b Sarwan	46		
†CMW Read	c Hinds	b Best	20		
AF Giles		b Sanford	27		
MJ Hoggard	not out		9		
SP Jones	c Sanford	b Hinds	7		
SJ Harmison	run out (Hinds)		13		
Extras	(b 7, lb 28, w 7, nb 18)		60	(b 1, nb 2)	3
TOTAL	(all out)		339	(for 0 wickets)	20

1/28, 2/33, 3/152, 4/194, 5/209
6/268, 7/278, 8/313, 9/325, 10/339

Bowling: *First Innings:* Collymore 26–7–55–0, Edwards 19.3–3–72–3, Best 19–1–57–1, Sanford 22–1–90–1, Hinds 11.5–2–18–1, Gayle 1–0–6–0, Sarwan 4–1–6–1. *Second Innings:* Best 1.3–0–8–0, Hinds 1–0–11–0.

III

ECB MOVES TO DETER STREAKING

On 17 May 2002, would-be streakers, who had previously felt confident that baring all would only result in them being kicked out of the ground, were informed by the England and Wales Cricket Board that in future such actions would result in their arrest and the possibility of a criminal record.

"Cricket in England got a big wake-up call last year. Although streakers appear to offer no obvious threat, players and officials do see them as illegal trespassers. We cannot differentiate between streakers, autograph hunters or the more threatening pitch invaders," said Warren Deutrom, Events Manager for the ECB.

AUSSIE BARBER FOXED

The Bedser twins were both in the England party that toured Australia in 1946. On one of their days off Alec visited a barber's shop in Sydney and had his hair cut. When he told his brother what he had done, Eric visited the same barber's shop shortly afterwards. A bewildered barber exclaimed: "Strike me, mate. I've just cut your bloody hair!" Without hesitation Eric replied: "Yes, I know. It's the stuff that you put on it that made it grow so fast."

THE FOUR MUSKETEERS

Only four players have scored 30,000 runs and taken 2,000 wickets in their careers: W. G. Grace, Frank Woolley, George Hirst and Wilfred Rhodes. Only Hirst and Rhodes have scored 20,000 runs and taken 2,000 wickets in the County Championship.

TOP OPENER AND TAIL-ENDER

Wilfred Rhodes shared in a stand of 323 with Sir Jack Hobbs at Melbourne in the fourth Test of the 1911/12 series. It is still the highest for England for the first wicket in an Ashes Test. Meanwhile his partnership of 130 with Tip Foster in the first Test at Sydney in 1903/04 is the highest last wicket stand for England in any Test match.

STUMP SMASHER

Patrick Patterson, the West Indies pace bowler, broke a stump in two with an exocet of a delivery to send England opener Tim Robinson walking at Jaipur in the 1987 World Cup.

III

INSCRIPTION ON THE ASHES URN

The gold plate on the Ashes urn is inscribed as follows:

> When Ivo goes back with the urn, the urn
> Studds, Steel and Tylecote return, return:
> The Welkin will ring loud.
> The great crowd will feel proud,
> Seeing Barlow and Bates with the urn, the urn;
> And the rest coming home with the urn.

LAMB CHOPS FOR RUNS

In his benefit season, David Steele persuaded a Northampton butcher to give him a lamb chop for every run he scored during the year. Steele had a fine season and the butcher owed him 1,756 lamb chops by the end of it!

MOST CENTURIES IN A TEST MATCH

A remarkable total of seven Test centuries were recorded by England and Australia at Trent Bridge in 1938, a feat equalled by the West Indies and Australia in Kingston in 1954/55.

BEDSER OVER THE BOUNDARY

In his 21-year career, Alec Bedser only left the field of play once while play was in progress – in a Test match against Australia in Adelaide during a heatwave. He felt ill, went to the boundary and then returned to carry on bowling.

MIKE HENDRICK

Mike Hendrick appeared in 30 Test matches for England between 1974 and 1981 as a right-arm fast-medium bowler. He took 87 wickets at an average of 25.84, and his best figures were 4 for 28 against India at Birmingham in 1974.

ENGLAND SMACKED ABOUT

In 1884 Australia's Percy McDonnell became the first batsman in Test history to score a century in each of two consecutive Test innings. He performed his feat against England.

III

ATHERTON FINED FOR BALL TAMPERING

During the first Test against South Africa at Lord's in July 1994, England captain Michael Atherton was caught on cameras seemingly rubbing something onto the ball before passing it back to the bowler. Atherton later admitted having had dirt in his pocket, but it was there to keep his hands dry whilst handling a ball they were trying to reverse-swing, but he denied having cheated. Chariman of selectors Ray Illingworth fined his captain £2,000.

TIMED OUT

Harold John Heygate played for the Epsom College XI and also occasionally turned out for Sussex in 1903 and 1905. He was a sound, stylish batsman who was once given out "timed out". In accordance with the laws of the day, it meant that the team's entire innings had come to an end.

MOST RUNS SCORED OFF ONE BALL

England's Patsy Hendren shares the record for the most runs scored off one ball, eight. England were playing in the first Test of the 1928/29 series against Australia at Brisbane. He hit a ball towards the boundary, but the Australians, in attempting to run him out going for a fourth, overthrew the ball to the boundary, giving him an 8. New Zealand's John Wright equalled the feat, in similar circumstances, also against Australia, in the third Test at Melbourne in December 1980.

LAKER'S TEST MATCH BOWLING RECORD

Jim Laker of England holds the distinction of possessing the best bowling figures in a Test Match. In the 1956 Ashes Test at Old Trafford he took 9 Australian wickets for 37 in the first innings and 10 for 53 in the second, giving him record match figures of 19 wickets for 90 runs. The only Australian wicket he failed to take was that of Burke, which was taken by Tony Lock. Anil Kumble of India is the only other bowler to take all 10 wickets in a Test innings. In the 1956 series, in which England retained the Ashes, Laker took an incredible 46 Australian wickets, a record for an Ashes series, at an average of 9.60.[†]

[†]In that 1956 summer Laker also took all 10 Australian wickets for just 88 runs when the tourists played Surrey.

III

⎯⟋ ASHES BOWLING MIX-UP ⟍⎯

During the 1921 Ashes series declarations had just been introduced in Test cricket, but the rules stated that a team was not permitted to declare on the first day if less than 100 minutes of play remained. In the fourth Test of the series the first day was washed out, and on the second day the England captain, Lionel Tennyson, wanted to declare but the Australian captain, Warwick Armstrong, claimed England could not declare since effectively it was still the first day. A 25-minute argument ensued, and neither of the umpires noticed that Armstrong bowled the last over before the hold-up and the first over immediately following it!

⎯⟋ AUSSIES ANNIHILATED ⟍⎯

England annihilated Australia in the fourth Test played at The Oval in August 1938 by an innings and 579 runs. The result occurred under Don Bradman's captaincy of Australia, but the legend did not bat in either innings, having been injured while bowling in the first Test. England made 903 for 7, with Len Hutton scoring 364.

⎯⟋ PLACE YOUR BETS ⟍⎯

The popularity of cricket as a game for wagers spread rapidly amongst the ruling class after 1735, when HRH Frederick Louis, Prince of Wales, played it for the first time in Kensington Gardens.

⎯⟋ COMPTON SCORES AT WEMBLEY ⟍⎯

During World War II, football in England was played on a regional basis, and in season 1940/41 Preston North End won the Northern Section Championship and also reached the final of the Wartime Cup. In the final Preston met Arsenal at Wembley and the game ended in a 1–1 draw, Arsenal's equalizer being scored by the England cricketer Denis Compton. Preston won the replay 2–1.

⎯⟋ PEACE DEAL OVER PACKER'S CIRCUS ⟍⎯

Prior to the 1979 World Cup finals, Kerry Packer and his "Cricket Circus" had split the cricket world. A truce was called just before the tournament and whereas England and Australia elected not to field their "Packer players", all of the other competing nations were at full strength.

⫿⫿

⌁ THE ASHES ⌁

England first played Australia in a Test match in 1877, but it wasn't until Australia beat England for the first time on English soil on 29th August 1882 that the rivalry between England and Australia became known as "the Ashes". The name comes from a fake obituary notice published in the *Sporting Times* on 30 August 1882. The obituary read:

> In Affectionate Remembrance of
> **English Cricket**
> which died at the Oval on
> 29th August, 1882.
> Deeply lamented by the large circle of
> sorrowing friends and acquaintances.
> R.I.P.
> NB – The body will be cremated and
> the Ashes taken to Australia.

A few weeks later, an English team, captained by the Honourable Ivo Bligh (later Lord Darnley), set off on a tour of Australia. England lost the first of the three scheduled Test matches but won the next two, prompting a group of Melbourne ladies, led by Miss Florence Rose Morphy, to burn one of the bails used in the third Test, place the ashes from it in a small brown urn, and present the urn to Bligh. The urn was taken back to England by Bligh, who considered the Ashes as a personal gift and retained them at his family home, Cobham Hall, at Rochester in Kent. In February 1884, Bligh married Miss Morphy. When he died in 1927, Bligh's widow bequeathed the Ashes to the MCC. Today, over 78 years later, this tiny and extremely delicate urn is visited at Lord's by tens of thousands of visitors from all over the world.

Australian cricket fans demanded that the urn return with their team after successful defences in 1993 and 1997, but the MCC refused to part with it, although a replica was made. However, after discussions with the England & Wales Cricket Board (ECB) and Cricket Australia, the MCC commissioned the Waterford Crystal Trophy, shaped like the Ashes urn. This was first presented to Australia's captain, Mark Taylor, after his team won the 1998/99 series. Since then, the Waterford Trophy has been presented to the winning captain at the end of each Ashes series, with Michael Vaughan the proud recipient in 2005. The original urn stands in the Memorial Gallery at Lord's.

III

FANTASY ENGLAND XI (16)

WARWICKSHIRE

1. *Dennis* AMISS
2. *Ron* BARBER
3. *Mike (M.J.K.)* SMITH *(CAPTAIN)*
4. *John* JAMESON
5. *Ian* BELL
6. *Nick* KNIGHT
7. *Dick* LILLEY *(WICKET-KEEPER)*
8. *Tom* CARTWRIGHT
9. *Ashley* GILES
10. *Gladstone* SMALL
11. *Bob* WILLIS
12th Man *Dermot* REEVE

Did You Know That?

Warwickshire CCC joined the County Championship in 1895 with three others, Derbyshire, Essex and Hampshire. The County plays its home games at Edgbaston, Birmingham. Warwickshire has won the County Championship six times (1911, 1951, 1972, 1994, 1995 and 2004).

ASHES FEVER (16)

"If we don't beat you, we'll knock your bloody heads off."
Bill Voce, England paceman, exchanges a friendly word with opponent Vic Richardson at the start of the fateful "Bodyline" Ashes series of 1932/33

THE GENTLE GIANT

David Larter enjoyed a very successful Test debut, taking nine wickets. The match, the fifth Test against Pakistan at The Oval, from 16 to 20 August 1962, saw the six foot, seven inch fast bowler take 5 for 57 in the first innings and 4 for 88 in the second. England won by 10 wickets.

ALLEN'S LONG SLOG

In 1902, Bobby Allen played a record number of first-class matches in a season, 41.

Ⅲ

∽ THE GREAT TEST MATCHES (12) ∾

England held their nerve on the fourth morning of the second Test at Edgbaston in 2005 to win the closest Test match in Ashes history by two runs. Two moments before play started on day one helped England: first Glenn McGrath put himself out of the match when he injured an ankle during the warm-ups by stepping on a ball lying in the outfield; then Ricky Ponting elected to field on winning the toss. It was an amazing decision, especially with McGrath absent, Jason Gillespie horribly out of form and Michael Kasprowicz a little rusty. Australia did bowl out England on the opening day, but at a cost of 407 runs – a scoring rate of 5.14 runs per over, which was almost of limited-over proportions. Marcus Trescothick with 90 and Andrew Strauss with 48 put on 116 for the first wicket. Kevin Pietersen and Andrew Flintoff both hit half-centuries, while Shane Warne replied for Australia with four wickets.

Day two saw Australia dismissed for 308 in 76 overs, despite 82 from Justin Langer, 61 from Ponting and forties from both Michael Clarke and Adam Gilchrist. Of the rest, only Damien Martyn even reached double figures. England's first innings lead of 99 was extended slightly, but the exaggerated turn of a ball from Shane Warne that bowled Strauss just before stumps set the England alarm bells ringing.

Andrew Flintoff, batting with a damaged shoulder on day three, gave England a chance. He smote six fours and four sixes and was last out for a brave 73 as England recovered from 75 for 6 and 131 for 9. They were finally bowled out for 182, Warne taking 6 for 46 and Brett Lee 4 for 82, setting Australia 282 to win. No team had ever achieved that total to win a Test at Edgbaston, but Australia seemed to be on their way when they reached 48 without loss just after tea. Enter Flintoff and, in his first over, exit Langer and Ponting. England took six more wickets before stumps, Clarke, the last recognized batsman, being yorked by a magnificent change-of-pace ball from Harmison with the final delivery of the day.

Edgbaston was packed for the denouement on the Sunday, even though the action might have lasted just two balls. Nobody really thought there was a chance of the Aussies getting the 107 runs they needed. But despite losing Warne, who trod on his stumps, at 220, Australia, with Lee and Michael Kasprowicz playing sensibly, edged ever closer. At 279, less than a boundary away from one of the greatest victories in cricket history, Harmison induced Kasprowicz to glove a ball to Geraint Jones. As his hand was off the bat, technically Kasprowicz should have been given not out, but Billy Bowden's crooked finger was raised and England had a two-run victory.

▥
ENGLAND V AUSTRALIA – Second Test
4–7 AUGUST 2005, EDGBASTON, BIRMINGHAM

Result: England won by 2 runs. *Toss:* Australia. *Umpires:* BF Bowden, RE Koertzen

ENGLAND

Batsman	First Innings			Second Innings		
ME Trescothick	c Gilchrist	b Kasprowicz	90	c Gilchrist	b Lee	21
AJ Strauss		b Warne	48		b Warne	6
*MP Vaughan	c Lee	b Gillespie	24	(4)	b Lee	1
IR Bell	c Gilchrist	b Kasprowicz	6	(5) c Gilchrist	b Warne	21
KP Pietersen	c Katich	b Lee	71	(6) c Gilchrist	b Warne	20
A Flintoff	c Gilchrist	b Gillespie	68	(7)	b Warne	73
†GO Jones	c Gilchrist	b Kasprowicz	1	(8) c Ponting	b Lee	9
AF Giles	lbw	b Warne	23	(9) c Hayden	b Warne	8
MJ Hoggard	lbw	b Warne	16	(3) c Hayden	b Lee	1
SJ Harmison		b Warne	17	c Ponting	b Warne	0
SP Jones	not out		19	not out		12
Extras	lb 9, w 1, nb 14		24	lb 1, nb 9		10
TOTAL	(all out)		407	(all out)		182

1/112, 2/164, 3/170, 4/187, 5/290

6/293, 7/342, 8/348, 9/375

1/25, 2/27, 3/29, 4/31, 5/72

6/75, 7/101, 8/131, 9/131

Bowling: *First Innings:* Lee 17–1–111–1, Gillespie 22–3–91–2, Kasprowicz 15–3–80–3, Warne25.2–4–116–4. *Second Innings:* Lee 18–1–82–4, Gillespie 8–0–24–0, Kasprowicz 3–0–29–0, Warne 23.1–7–46–6.

AUSTRALIA

Batsman	First Innings			Second Innings		
JL Langer	lbw	b SP Jones	82		b Flintoff	28
ML Hayden	c Strauss	b Hoggard	0	c Trescothick	b SP Jones	31
*RT Ponting	c Vaughan	b Giles	61	c GO Jones	b Flintoff	0
DR Martyn	run out (Vaughan)		20	c Bell	b Hoggard	28
MJ Clarke	c GO Jones	b Giles	40		b Harmison	30
SM Katich	c GO Jones	b Flintoff	4	c Trescothick	b Giles	16
†AC Gilchrist	not out		49	c Flintoff	b Giles	1
SK Warne		b Giles	8	(9) c Hayden	b Flintoff	42
B Lee	c Flintoff	b SP Jones	6	(10) not out		43
JN Gillespie	lbw	b Flintoff	7	(8)	b Flintoff	0
MS Kasprowicz	lbw	b Flintoff	0	c GO Jones	b Harmison	20
Extras	b 13, lb 7, nb 10, w 1		31	b 13, lb 8, nb 18, w 1		40
TOTAL	(all out)		308	(all out)		279

1/0, 2/88, 3/118, 4/194, 5/208

6/262, 7/273, 8/282, 9/308

1/47, 2/48, 3/82, 4/107, 5/134

6/136, 7/137, 8/175, 9/220

Bowling: *First Innings:* Harmison 11–1–48–0, Hoggard 8–0–41–1, SP Jones 16–2–69–2, Flintoff 15–1–52–3, Giles 15–3–68–2. *Second Innings:* Harmison 17.3–3–62–2, Hoggard 5–0–26–1, Flintoff 22–3–79–4, Giles 26–2–78–3, SP Jones 5–1–23–1.

⚏

⟿ SIR LEONARD HUTTON ⟿

Leonard Hutton was born on 23 June 1916 in Fulneck, Yorkshire. As a boy, Hutton, who was from a keen cricketing family, watched players such as Wilfred Rhodes, Herbert Sutcliffe and Bill Bowes. He made his first-class debut for Yorkshire in 1934, aged 17, and he scored five fifties and his maiden first-class century in 14 County Championship matches that season. He could bat on all types of surfaces, displaying his artistry with the bat on the uncovered wickets of that era.

In 1937 Hutton made his Test debut against New Zealand and, in his second Test, scored his first century at Old Trafford. A year later broke the legendary Don Bradman's highest individual score in a Test match with 364. He achieved this remarkable record against Australia at The Oval, completing it in 13 hours at the crease. In 1939 he tore the West Indies attack apart, scoring 196 at Lord's with his final 96 runs coming in 95 minutes. When war broke out in 1939, Hutton was recruited as a Physical Training Instructor in the Army. In a freak accident in the gym he broke his left arm so badly that he had to have bone grafts to repair the damage. It ended up two inches shorter than his right.

Although he played in the first post-war series against Australia in 1946/47, scoring a century in the last Test, Hutton was controversially dropped in 1948 for the home series against Australia, only to be restored to the team after a public outcry. During the 1950s he established himself as England's leading batsman. In the 1950 Oval Test against the West Indies spinners he scored 202 not out and in 1952 he was appointed England captain. That year Hutton led England to victory over India, and in 1953 he helped England regain the Ashes from Lindsay Hassett's team. England went 2–0 down against the West Indies in 1953/54, but Hutton rallied the team to draw the series.

In the 1954/55 Ashes series Hutton once again showed his outstanding leadership abilities after England had been torn apart by the Australians in Brisbane. England retained the Ashes, winning the series 3–1. That Ashes triumph proved to be his curtain call as far as Test cricket was concerned, as he had to withdraw from England's following series through ill health. In 1956 he retired, having played 79 Test matches, scoring 6,971 runs at an average of 56.67, with 19 centuries. He amassed 40,140 runs in first-class cricket at an average of 55.51, with 129 centuries. A proud Yorkshireman, in 1956 he was knighted for his services to cricket. Sir Leonard Hutton died on 6 September 1990.

♟ HIGHEST TEST PARTNERSHIP RECORDS ♟

Only one England stand appears in the table for the highest partnerships in Test cricket for each wicket:

Ptnrshp	Runs	Players	Opponents	Venue/Year
1st	413	Vinoo Mankad & Pankaj Roy (IND)	v New Zealand	Chennai 1955/56
2nd	576†	Sanath Jayasuriya & Roshan Mahanama (SL)	v India	Colombo 1997/98
3rd	467	Andrew Jones & Martin Crowe (NZ)	v Sri Lanka	Wellington 1990/91
4th	411	Peter May & Colin Cowdrey (ENG)	v West Indies	Birmingham 1957
5th	405	Sid Barnes & Don Bradman (AUS)	v England	Sydney 1946/47
6th	346	Jack Fingleton & Don Bradman (AUS)	v England	Melbourne 1936/37
7th	347	Denis Atkinson & Clairmonte Depeiaza (WI)	v Australia	Bridgetown 1954/55
8th	313	Wasim Akram & Saqlain Mushtaq (PAK)	v Zimbabwe	Sheikhupura 1996/97
9th	195	Mark Boucher & Pat Symcox (SA)	v Pakistan	Johannesburg 1997/98
10th	151	Azhar Mahmood & Mushtaq Ahmed (PAK)	v South Africa	Auckland 1997/98
10th	151	Brian Hastings & Richard Collinge (NZ)	v Pakistan	Rawalpindi 1972/73

†Sri Lanka made a Test record score of 952-6 declared in this match with Jayasuriya scoring 340, Mahanama 225 and Aravinda da Silva 126.

♟ AMAZING GRACE ♟

In 1878, at the Kennington Oval, W.G. Grace threw a cricket ball over 116 yards (106m) three times assisted by the wind and 100 yards against the wind.

♟ A PROFESSIONAL CAPTAIN ♟

Len Hutton was made England captain in 1952, thus becoming the first professional skipper of the country. All of his predecessors had been amateurs.

III

"[The Queen] was saying she watched the series avidly – but not all the time, because it all got a bit too tense for her and was a bit nerve-wracking."

Michael Vaughan *describes his conversation with Her Majesty when he went to Buckingham Palace to collect his OBE*

─◦ LORD COWDREY ◦─

Former England captain Colin Cowdrey was a prominent member of the Conservative Party and was a close friend of Prime Minister John Major. In 1997 John Major made him Lord Cowdrey of Tonbridge.

─◦ MASSIE BOWLS ENGLAND OVER ◦─

Bob Massie of Australia made one of the most dramatic impacts in Test cricket history when he made his Test debut against England in the Second Test of the 1972 Ashes Series at Lord's. The fast-medium swing bowler took eight English wickets for 84 runs in the first innings and a further eight wickets for 53 runs in England's second innings. His debut figures of 16 wickets for 137 runs were the best by a Test debutant until India's Narendra Hirwani took 16 West Indian wickets for only 136 runs in January 1988. However, Massie only played in five more Tests for his country, making his last Test appearance against Pakistan in Sydney in January 1973, and eighteen months after his demolition of England, he was dropped by his State side, Western Australia

Did You Know That?
Bob Massie was a banker by profession but after his cricket career ended he turned to radio commentary.

─◦ LARA PUTS ENGLAND TO THE SWORD ◦─

West Indies batsman Brian Lara has recorded two of the three highest ever individual Test scores, and he achieved both of them against England. Lara's record score of 375 from 1994 was briefly surpassed in 2003 by Australia's Matthew Hayden, but he grabbed back top spot six months later with England again the victims:

1. 400* Brian Lara, West Indies v England, St John's, 2003/04
2. 380 Matthew Hayden, Australia v Zimbabwe, Perth, 2003/04
3. 375 Brian Lara, West Indies v England, St John's, 1993/94

II

─◦ THE YOUNG CRICKETER OF THE YEAR ◦─

The winners of the Cricket Writers' Club Award for the Young Cricketer of the Year:

1950	Roy Tattersall	1979	Paul Parker
1951	Peter May	1980	Bill Athey,
1952	Fred Trueman		Graham Dilley
1953	Colin Cowdrey	1981	Mike Gatting
1954	Peter Loader	1982	Norman Cowans
1955	Ken Barrington	1983	Neil Foster
1956	Brian Taylor	1984	Rob Bailey
1957	Micky Stewart	1985	David Lawrence
1958	Colin Ingleby-Mackenzie	1986	Ashley Metcalfe,
1959	Geoff Pullar		James Whitaker
1960	David Allen	1987	Richard Blakey
1961	Peter Parfitt	1988	Matthew Maynard
1962	Phil Sharpe	1989	Nasser Hussain
1963	Geoff Boycott	1990	Michael Atherton
1964	Mike Brearley	1991	Mark Ramprakash
1965	Alan Knott	1992	Ian Salisbury
1966	Derek Underwood	1993	Mark Lathwell
1967	Tony Greig	1994	John Crawley
1968	Bob Cottam	1995	Andrew Symonds
1969	Alan Ward	1996	Chris Silverwood
1970	Chris Old	1997	Ben Hollioake
1971	John Whitehouse	1998	Andrew Flintoff
1972	Dudley Owen-Thomas	1999	Alex Tudor
1973	Mike Hendrick	2000	Paul Franks
1974	Phil Edmonds	2001	Owais Shah
1975	Andrew Kennedy	2002	Rikki Clarke
1976	Geoff Miller	2003	James Anderson
1977	Ian Botham	2004	Ian Bell
1978	David Gower	2005	Alastair Cook

─◦ THORPE'S ROYAL TREAT ◦─

On 17 June 2006, Graham Thorpe, who played in 100 Tests and 82 ODIs for England, was awarded an MBE in the Queen's 80th Birthday Honours list. Thorpe, who represented England between 1993 and 2002, racked up 16 centuries, 39 half-centuries and had a top score of 200 not out – against New Zealand in Christchurch in March 2002 – during his Test career.

III

~ FANTASY ENGLAND XI (17) ~

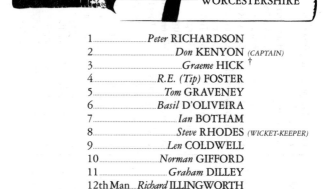

WORCESTERSHIRE

1.................................*Peter* RICHARDSON
2.................................*Don* KENYON *(CAPTAIN)*
3.................................*Graeme* HICK †
4.................................*R.E. (Tip)* FOSTER
5.................................*Tom* GRAVENEY
6.................................*Basil* D'OLIVEIRA
7.................................*Ian* BOTHAM
8.................................*Steve* RHODES *(WICKET-KEEPER)*
9.................................*Len* COLDWELL
10...............................*Norman* GIFFORD
11...............................*Graham* DILLEY
12th Man....*Richard* ILLINGWORTH

Did You Know That?

Worcestershire CCC was formed on 11 March 1865 and attained first-class status in 1899. The County play its home games at New Road, Worcester, and has won the County Championship five times (1964, 1965, 1974, 1988 and 1989).

~ E.W. SWANTON ~

Jim Swanton, a former Middlesex cricketer and one of the most influential cricket writers of the 20th century (for The Daily Telegraph) dined with the high and mighty including prime ministers and high commissioners, leading his colleagues to comment: "Jim is such a snob that he won't travel in the same car as his chauffeur!"

The election of a new Pope was taking place in Rome as the conclave of cardinals met at the Vatican. A huge crowd was waiting in St Peter's Square in anticipation of a puff of white smoke signalling a new Pope had been elected. At the same time a Test match was taking place at Lord's with Brian Johnston commentating. When Johnston saw one of the chimneys of the Old Tavern belching smoke the television cameras panned on the chimney, as Johnston quipped: "Ah, I see that Jim Swanton has just been elected Pope!"

† *Graeme Hick hit his 100th century for Worcestershire in June 2006, becoming only the eighth player in English cricket history to score a century of centuries for the same county.*

⚬ ENGLAND CRICKETING NICKNAMES ⚬

Bobby Abel — The Guv'nor
Jonathan Agnew — Aggers
Sir George Allen — Gubby
Mark Alleyne — BooBoo
James Anderson — Jimmy Boy
Geoff Arnold — Horse
Michael Atherton — Athers
Trevor Bailey — The Boil
Ian Bell — Belly
Harold Bird — Dickie
Henry Blofeld — Blowers
Ian Botham — Beefy
Andy Caddick — Caddyshack
Paul Collingwood — Colly
Colin Cowdrey — Kipper
Phillip DeFreitas — Daffy
Graham Dilley — Pica
J.W.H.T. Douglas — Johnny Won't Hit Today
Keith Fletcher — The Gnome of Essex
Andrew Flintoff — Freddie
James Foster — The Child

Graeme Fowler — Foxy
C. B. Fry — Lord Oxford
Ashley Giles — Ash
Graham Gooch — Zap
Darren Gough — Rhino
Sir Henry Leveson-Gower — Shrimp
E. M. Grace — The Coroner
W.G. Grace — The Doctor
Stephen Harmison — Harmy
Sir Jack Hobbs — The Master
Matthew Hoggard — Hoggy
Albert Hornby — Monkey
Simon Hughes — Yozzer
Nasser Hussain — Nass
Bert Ironmonger — Dainty
Gilbert Jessop — The Croucher
Harold Larwood — Lol
David Lloyd — Bumble
Charles Marriott — Father Marriott
Chris Old — Chilly
Monty Panesar — The Mont-ster
Kevin Pietersen — KP

Mark Ramprakash — Bloodaxe
Kumar Shri Ranjitsinhji — Black Prince of Cricketers
Derek Randall — Arkle
Harold Rhodes — Dusty Rhodes
Sir Aubrey Smith — Round the Corner
Jim Smith — Big Jim
Brian Statham — George
Edward Stevens — Lumpy
Alec Stewart — Wizenedone
Andrew Strauss — Lord Brocket
Graham Thorpe — The Shagger
Marcus Trescothick — Banger
Fred Trueman — Fiery Fred
Phil Tufnell — The Cat
Frank Tyson — Typhoon
Shaun Udal — Shaggy
Derek Underwood — Deadly
Michael Vaughan — Virgil
Sir Pelham Warner — Plum Warner
Craig White — Chalky

⫶

⊸ FAMOUS CRICKETING GAFFES ⟣⟢

Michael Holding of the West Indies was bowling to England's Peter Willey when *Brian Johnston* came out with perhaps cricket's most famous line of commentary: "The bowler's Holding, the batsman's Willey".

In 1962 Pakistan toured England and Barry Knight was batting for England when *Rex Alston* said: "There is a bowling change and we are going to see A. Fagge [a fag] at the Nursery End."

At Headingley in 1961, Harvey was fielding at leg slip. *Brian Johnston* was the commentator and said: "Harvey is waiting with his legs wide apart, waiting for a tickle."

"As you come over, Ray Illingworth has just relieved himself at the pavilion end." *Brian Johnston*

In July 1969, Alan Ward made his England Test debut against New Zealand at Lord's. With the fifth ball of an over, he struck Glen Turner a nasty blow on the box. After a few minutes Turner staggered back to the crease, at which point *Brian Johnston* said: "It looks as if he is going to try to continue. Very plucky of him. One ball left!"

South Africa's Peter Pollock was playing for the Rest of the World when he slipped and twisted his ankle. *Brian Johnston* commentating on the match with Denis Compton said: "He [Pollock] is in excruciating pain. It is especially bad, as he is here on his honeymoon with his pretty wife. Still he'll probably be all right tomorrow, if he sticks it up tonight." Denis Compton rolled about the commentary box in stitches.

On a visit to the Middle East, *Freddie Truman* learnt that his host had 198 wives. According to John Arlott, Freddie is supposed to have said: "Golly, another two and he can claim the new ball!"

The irrepressible *Ian Botham* once quipped: "Pakistan is the sort of place every man should send his mother-in-law, for a month, with all expenses paid" after he returned early from a tour of Pakistan during the 1980s. However, when Pakistan beat England in the 1992 World Cup final Aamer Sohail took some revenge as he told Botham: "Why don't you send your mother-in-law out to play, she cannot do much worse."

III

ENGLAND JOY RIDERS

During the 1990/91 Ashes tour of Australia David Gower and team-mate John Morris decided to have a bit of fun when England were four down (Gower and Morris were both out before lunch with Morris scoring a century) in a match against Queensland at the Carrara Oval, a stadium situated on Australia's Gold Coast approximately 50 miles from Brisbane. Gower and Morris paid a visit to a nearby airfield at the break and after checking that Allan Lamb and Robin Smith were still batting Gower and Morris each hired a pre-war Tiger Moth plane from a company named "Joy Rides".

The planes were required to fly at a minimum height of 2,000 feet but Gower persuaded his pilot to do a spot of low flying as they flew across the Oval closer to 200 feet. The England pair buzzed the ground just minutes after Smith completed his century whilst Lamb, who knew his team-mates were in the planes, playfully pretended to shoot them down with his bat.

When the flying aces got back to the dressing-room, Gooch asked them if they were in the planes that raced over his head to which Gower said no. The incident almost resulted in the pair being sent home after the local press got hold of the story but in the end they got a severe ticking off from the England management team and a fine of £1,000 each, the maximum allowed under their contracts.

GIVE ME ARTHUR

Arthur Shrewsbury was born on 11 April 1856 in New Lenton, Nottinghamshire. Shrewsbury, who played for Nottingham and participated in 23 Test matches for England, captaining the side seven times (5 wins, 2 losses) was one of the most dominant batsmen from the Victorian era and rivalled even the legendary WG Grace. Indeed, when Grace himself was once asked who he would pick first for his side simply replied "Give Me Arthur". Shrewsbury was voted Wisden Cricketer of the Year in 1890 and retired from playing in 1902. In 1903, following a bout of depression he committed suicide by shooting himself at his sister's home in Gedling, Nottinghamshire after mistakenly believing he was suffering from an incurable disease.

Did You Know That?
William Scotton, a team-mate of Arthur Shrewsbury, committed suicide on 9 July 1893 following a bout of depression after losing his place in the Nottinghamshire team in 1891.

Ⅲ

The fourth Test of the 2005 Ashes series was played at Trent Bridge, Nottingham, from 25 to 29 August 2005. The series was tied at 1–1 following the visitors' fight back at Old Trafford to deny England victory. England won the toss and decided to bat.

By close of play on the first day England had scored 229 for 4 (Kevin Pietersen 33 not out and Andrew Flintoff 8 not out). On the second day Flintoff reached his century (102, including 14 fours and a six) before succumbing lbw to Shaun Tait, and wicket-keeper Geraint Jones chipped in with 85 as England reached 477. Australia then slipped to 99 for 5 at the close.

Australia were all out for 218 on day three and, trailing England by 259 runs, were asked to follow on in a Test match for the first time since the early days of Allan Border's captaincy. The Aussies fought hard and ended the third day's play on 222 for 4 (Michael Clarke 39 not out and Simon Katich 24 not out).

England finally bowled Australia out for 337 to set themselves a nerve-jangling 129 runs for victory. England looked fine until Warne was introduced, then suddenly things began to unravel. Thirty-two for no wicket became 57 for 4 as the magician went through his tricks. Pietersen and Flintoff steadied the ship, only for the former to edge behind off Lee and Freddie to get a brute of a ball from the same bowler that rocketed through his defences. When Geraint Jones tried to loft Warne into the stands and instead found Michael Kasprowicz, England were 116 for 7. Ashley Giles – no mug with the bat – was joined by Matthew Hoggard, with only Harmison and an injured Simon Jones to come.

England edged towards their target, while the Australian bowlers smelled blood and a win that would mean they retained the Ashes. Striving for the yorker, Brett Lee gave Hoggard a full toss outside off-stump that the Yorkshireman sent racing to the cover boundary, relieving the pressure. Next over, Giles worked Warne into the leg side and set off on the runs that gave England victory. England were in the driving seat, leading the series 2–1, and believing that they could reclaim the Ashes. All would be decided at The Oval.

Did You Know That?

Trent Bridge, which is actually in West Bridgeford, Nottinghamshire, hosted its inaugural Test match in 1899. In its early years the ground was shared by Nottinghamshire County Cricket Club and Notts County Football Club. However, in 1910 Notts County moved back across the River Trent, into the city, to Meadow Lane.

▥

ENGLAND V AUSTRALIA – Fourth Test
25–29 AUGUST 2005, TRENT BRIDGE, NOTTINGHAM
Result: England won by 3 wickets. *Toss:* England. *Umpires:* Aleem Dar. SA Bucknor.

ENGLAND

ME Trescothick		b Tait	65	c Ponting	b Warne	27
AJ Strauss	c Hayden	b Warne	35	c Clarke	b Warne	23
*MP Vaughan	c Gilchrist	b Ponting	58	c Hayden	b Warne	0
IR Bell	c Gilchrist	b Tait	3	c Kasprowicz	b Lee	3
KP Pietersen	c Gilchrist	b Lee	45	c Gilchrist	b Lee	23
A Flintoff	lbw	b Tait	102		b Lee	26
†GO Jones	c & b	Kasprowicz	85	c Kasprowicz	b Warne	3
AF Giles	lbew	b Warne	15	not out		7
MJ Hoggard	c Gilchrist	b Warne	10	not out		8
SJ Harmison	st Gilchrist	b Warne	2			
SP Jones	not out		15			
Extras	(b 1, lb 15, w 1, nb 25)		42	(lb 4, nb 5)		9
TOTAL	(all out)		477	(for 7 wickets)		129

1/105, 2/137, 3/146, 4/213, 5/241
6/418, 7/450, 8/450, 9/454, 10/477

1/32, 2/36. 3//57, 4/57, 5/103
6/111, 7/116

Bowling: *First Innings:* Lee 32–1–131– 1, Kasprowicz 32–3–122–1, Tait 24–4–97–3, Warne 29.1–4–102–4, Ponting 6–2–9–1. *Second Innings:* Lee 12–0–51–3, Kasprowicz 2–0–19–0, Warne 13.5–2–31–4, Tait 4–0–24–0.

AUSTRALIA

JL Langer	c Bell	b Hoggard	28	c Bell	b Giles	61
ML Hayden	lbw	b Hoggard	7	c Giles	b Flintoff	26
*RT Ponting	lbw	b SP Jones	1	run out (sub GJ Pratt)		48
DR Martyn	lbw	b Hoggard	1	c GO Jones	b Flintoff	13
MJ Clarke	lbw	b Harmison	36	c GO Jones	b Hoggard	56
SM Katich	c Strauss	b SP Jones	45	lbw	b Harmison	59
†AC Gilchrist	c Strauss	b Flintoff	27	lbw	b Hoggard	11
SK Warne	c Bell	b SP Jones	0	st GO Jones	b Giles	45
B Lee	c Bell	b SP Jones	47	not out		26
MS Kasprowicz		b SP Jones	5	c GO Jones	b Harmison	19
SW Tait	not out		3		b Harmison	4
Extras	(lb 2, w 1, nb 16)		19	(b 1, lb 4, nb 14)		19
TOTAL	(all out)		218	(all out)		387

1/2, 2/21, 3/22, 4/58, 5/99
6/157, 7/157, 8/163, 9/175, 10/218

1/50, 2/129, 3/155, 4/161, 5/261
6/277, 7/314, 8/342, 9/373, 10/387

Bowling: *First Innings:* Harmison 9–1–48–1, Hoggard 15–3–70–3, SP Jones 14.1–4–44–5, Flintoff 11–1–55–1. *Second Innings:* Hoggard 27–7–72–2, SP Jones 4–0–15–0, Harmison 30–5–93–3, Flintoff 29–4–83–2, Giles 28–3–107–2, Bell 6–2–12–0.

III

"But to suggest I got out, as some people did, because I had tears in my eyes is to belittle the bowler and is quite untrue."
Don Bradman *on his duck in his last Test (1948).*

~⟶ GEORGE DAVIS IS INNOCENT ⟵~

On 19 August 1975, campaigners calling for the release of George Davis from prison vandalised the pitch at Headingley during the third test of an Ashes series. Davis was an east London minicab driver who was jailed for 20 years for his part in an armed robbery. His supporters dug holes in the pitch and poured oil over one end of the wicket. The walls surrounding Headingley were painted with the slogan: "G. DAVIS IS INNOCENT". The damage to the pitch resulted in the final match between England and Australia being abandoned. The Test was declared a draw and deprived England of the opportunity of winning back the Ashes.

Did You Know That?
After the Headingley incident an internal enquiry was set up to investigate the way the Metropolitan Police had handled Davis' case. In May 1976, Roy Jenkins, the Home Secretary, released Davis from prison after declaring that there was serious doubt about the evidence given by two police officers who had identified Davis as being involved in the robbery.

~⟶ SIR GEORGE'S LORD'S RECORD ⟵~

Sir George Allen holds the all-time Test record partnership for the eighth wicket, a score of 246 against New Zealand in 1931, along with Les Ames. Allen is also the only man ever to have taken all 10 wickets at Lord's, a feat he achieved for Middlesex in 1929 for a mere 40 runs against Lancashire.

~⟶ ENGLAND PLAYER ROW ⟵~

Raman Subba Row, who played county cricket for Surrey and Northamptonshire, played in 13 Tests for England between 1958 and 1961. Subba Row was a left-handed batsman and hit a century in his first Ashes Test (112 at Edgbaston in 1961) and in his last Test against Australia (137 at The Oval, also in 1961). He was a Wisden Cricketer of the Year in 1961.

Ⅲ

⮎ JIM LAKER ⮌

James Charles Laker was born on 8th February 1922 in Frizinghall, Yorkshire. After playing twice for Surrey in 1946 against a Combined Services XI, the promising young spin bowler was taken on to the county staff after permission had been obtained from Yorkshire. At the end of the 1947 season he was selected for an experimental MCC side that Gubby Allen took to the West Indies. In the first innings of the first Test he took 7 for 103 and led the bowling averages for the tour.

In 1948, he was taught a lesson by the powerful Australian attack which visited England for the Ashes series. In his second appearance against Australia for the MCC at Lord's, he was hit for nine sixes on the second morning. He was still chosen for the first Ashes Test and starred for England by scoring 63 in his first innings, but in the second Test he was lacklustre. He was dropped when the third Test came around but then recalled for the fourth. His 14 wickets against the Australians came at a heavy cost, an average of 59.35, which led the selectors to cast doubts over his ability as a Test match bowler.

However, over the next few years he was a key player in the Surrey side which won the County Championship in seven successive seasons from 1952 to 1958. In 1950, he took 8 for 2 for England against "The Rest" at Bradford, but over the following six years he was often left out of the England team. However, he did secure victory for England in the final Test against South Africa in 1951 with 4 for 64 and 6 for 55, and after taking more than 100 wickets for Surrey that season he was included in *Wisden*'s Cricketers of the Year in 1952. In 1957 he played in four Tests against the West Indies, missing one through illness, and in 1958 he played in four of England's five Tests against New Zealand.

In 1956/57 he was a member of the MCC side that toured South Africa, and in 1958/59 he was chosen for the tour of Australia. At the end of the 1959 season he retired from cricket after taking 1,395 wickets at an average of 17.37 in 309 matches in 13 years. In eleven of the years he spent at Surrey he exceeded 100 wickets in a season. In 1962 he was persuaded by his close friend Trevor Bailey to play for Essex. Over the next three years he played in 30 matches for the county as an amateur.

In all first-class matches he took 1,944 wickets at an average of 18.41 and scored 7,304 runs at an average of 16.60, including two centuries, both for Surrey. In 46 Test matches, he took 193 wickets at an average of 21.24. In retirement, Laker became a respected commentator with the BBC. He died, aged 64, on 23 April 1986.

⫼

‑ BAD AWAY DAYS (6) ‑

England's tour of Zimbabwe, 2004

In February 2003, the England and Wales Cricket Board withdrew England from a forthcoming World Cup game against Zimbabwe in Harare over safety concerns. England were also due to tour Zimbabwe in late 2004, and in December 2003 Peter Chingoka, the head of the Zimbabwe Cricket Union, publicly stated that the ECB must honour their agreement to tour, prompting Jack Straw, the Foreign Secretary, to intervene. In January 2004, Straw supported the ECB's stance leading Chingoka to email all of the first-class counties warning them that legal action would be taken against them if England did not play in Harare with damages estimated at £1.1 million. In late January 2004, Ehsan Mani, the ICC president, said: "I think the reality is that England will not tour Zimbabwe in November." However, six weeks later Mani did a U-turn stating: "Touring teams are expected to fulfil their touring obligations." Amazingly, Tony Blair then entered the dispute in May 2004 claiming that the government could not force England to tour Zimbabwe.

On 10 June 2004, despite the ICC suspending Zimbabwe's Test status for the remainder of 2004, they still stated that England had to tour Zimbabwe in November. On 9 September 2004, the ECB issued a statement stating that England would play five one-day matches in Zimbabwe "in the absence of firm instruction from the government not to tour" and nineteen days later the squad was named. Andrew Flintoff and Marcus Trescothick would not be going as they needed rest whilst Michael Vaughan said he would lead the side. In November 2004, England travelled to Namibia to play two warm-up matches and yet more controversy followed when England cancelled their flight to Zimbabwe after learning that the BBC and four English newspapers were informed that their journalists would not be permitted into the country to report on the series. On 25 November 2004, the Zimbabwean government backed down after England threatened to boycott the tour and allowed the media into Zimbabwe. On 5 December 2004, England beat Zimbabwe in Bulawayo by 74 runs to complete a 4–0 whitewash (the first match was cancelled) and thus ending one of the most controversial tours in the history of cricket.

Did You Know That?

Marcus Trescothick was nicknamed Banger by his Somerset team-mates from an early age due to his love of sausages.

III

⤙ FANTASY ENGLAND XI (18) ⤚

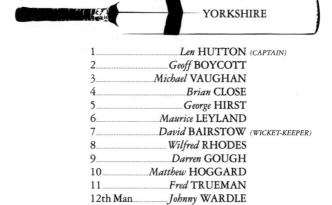

YORKSHIRE

1	*Len* HUTTON *(CAPTAIN)*
2	*Geoff* BOYCOTT
3	*Michael* VAUGHAN
4	*Brian* CLOSE
5	*George* HIRST
6	*Maurice* LEYLAND
7	*David* BAIRSTOW *(WICKET-KEEPER)*
8	*Wilfred* RHODES
9	*Darren* GOUGH
10	*Matthew* HOGGARD
11	*Fred* TRUEMAN
12th Man	*Johnny* WARDLE

Did You Know That?

Yorkshire CCC was founded on 8 January 1863 in the Adelphi Hotel, Sheffield, and up until 1893, it played its home games at Sheffield United Football Club's Bramall Lane ground. In 1891, the club moved its headquarters to Headingley. Yorkshire have won the County Championship outright a record 30 times (and shared it once), 11 times more than their nearest challengers, Surrey.

⤙ TEN LORDS A'LEAPING ⤚

Hon. Ivo Francis Walter Bligh (8th Earl of Darnley) 1882–1883
Hon. Frederick Somerset Gough-Calthorpe 1930
Hon. Charles John Coventry 1888
Lord George Robert Canning Harris 1878–1884
Lord Martin Bladen Hawke (7th Baron Hawke) 1895–1898
Hon. Sir Stanley Jackson 1893–1905
Hon. Alfred Lyttelton 1880–1884
Sir Tim O'Brien (3rd Baronet) 1884–1896
Lord Lionel Hallam Tennyson 1913–1921
Lord Cowdrey of Tonbridge 1954–1975

Did You Know That?

The former England cricket captain and chairman of selectors, Ted Dexter is affectionately known as "Lord Ted".

☰

⚬ TOP 20 LEADING TEST WICKET-TAKERS ⚬

Bowler	M	Balls	Md	Runs	Wkts	Ave.	Best	5WI	10WM	S.R.
IT Botham	102	21,815	788	10,878	383	28.40	8-34	27	4	56.96
RGD Willis	90	17,357	554	8,190	325	25.20	8-43	16	-	53.41
FS Trueman	67	15,178	522	6,625	307	21.58	8-31	17	3	49.44
DL Underwood	86	21,862	1,239	7,674	297	25.84	8-51	17	6	73.61
JB Statham	70	16,056	595	6,261	252	24.85	7-39	9	1	63.71
AV Bedser	51	15,918	574	5,876	236	24.90	7-44	15	5	67.45
AR Caddick	62	13,558	500	6,999	234	29.91	7-46	13	1	57.94
D Gough	58	11,821	370	6,503	229	28.40	6-42	9	-	51.62
MJ Hoggard	54	11,340	418	6,134	212	28.93	7-61	6	1	53.49
JA Snow	49	12,021	415	5,387	202	26.67	7-40	8	1	59.51
JC Laker	46	12,027	674	4,101	193	21.25	10-53	9	3	62.32
SF Barnes	27	7,873	356	3,106	189	16.43	9-103	24	7	41.66
A Flintoff	61	11,536	402	5,720	179	31.95	5-58	2	-	64.44
ARC Fraser	46	10,876	439	4,836	177	27.32	8-53	13	2	61.45
GAR Lock	49	13,147	819	4,451	174	25.58	7-35	9	3	75.56
SJ Harmison	40	8,774	297	4,514	155	29.12	7-12	6	-	56.60
MW Tate	39	12,523	581	4,055	155	26.16	6-42	7	1	80.79
FJ Titmus	53	15,118	777	4,931	153	32.23	7-79	7	-	98.81
JE Emburey	64	15,391	741	5,646	147	38.41	7-78	6	-	104.70
H Verity	40	11,173	604	3,510	144	24.38	8-43	5	2	77.59

Up to and including the Test series v Sri Lanka in May/June 2006

Ⅲ

✧ ONE OF OUR BATSMEN IS MISSING ✧

David Steele nearly had the most embarrassing Test debut ever. Aged 34, he was called up by England to play in the second Test of the 1975 series against Australia at Lord's, starting on 31 July. Batting first, England lost opener Barry Wood, lbw to Denis Lillee, in the fifth over, signalling the arrival of Steele. The Northamptonshire batsman had carefully remembered how many flights of stairs there were from the home dressing-room in the pavilion to the main ground. Unfortunately, he miscalculated and instead of walking into the Long Room, he ended up in the members' toilets in the basement. He quickly ran back up the stairs, walked through the Long Room and out on to field in time. He had used up almost all of his allotted two minutes, but no Australian appealed, which was just as well for Steele, who went on to make a 50 in his first innings.

Did You Know That?
When David Steele finally took to the Lord's pitch to make his England debut, Australian bowler Jeff Thomson is reported to have said: "Who's this then? Father bloody Christmas?" Thomson later bowled Steele out.

✧ ASHES FEVER (19) ✧

"Neil [Harvey] was the finest left-hander I ever bowled against and in our many challenging duels in the past the honours had gone very much his way. But, as luck would have it this time, I managed to bowl him a beauty first ball. From around the wicket, I held it back sufficiently for the ball to drift in and pitch around the leg and middle stumps. It turned just enough to clip his off-stump."
Jim Laker describes the most-prized scalp of his 19-wicket haul against the Aussies at Old Trafford in 1956

✧ HOWZAT HOLLYWOOD? ✧

Sir Charles Aubrey Smith played in just one Test match for England, a game in which he was captain when England beat South Africa at Port Elizabeth in March 1889. After his cricket career ended, Smith went to Hollywood where he became a movie star and today his name can be found on the famous Hollywood Walk of Fame. Some of his movies include: Little Women, The Four Feathers, The Prisoner of Zenda and The Lives of a Bengal Lancer.

▥

∽ FIRST TWENTY/20 INTERNATIONAL ∾

On 13 June 2005, England played Australia for the very first time in a Twenty/20 match. The venue was the Rose Bowl, Southampton and England won the toss and decided to bat. England started well despite Andrew Flintoff exiting the field after only nine minutes and 6 runs but England soon progressed to 100 for 3 when Kevin Pietersen was bowled by Michael Clarke and caught by Matthew Hayden when he was on 34 runs. However, things gradually slipped away from the England batsmen as Michael Vaughan caught by Ricky Ponting off the bowling of Andrew Symonds with the very first ball he faced (102–4). England closed their innings on 179 runs for 8 wickets after 79 minutes and the permitted 20 overs. It looked a vulnerable score, but the England bowlers then ripped through the Australian batting with Gloucestershire's right arm medium-fast bowler Jonathan Lewis registering superb figures of 4 wickets for 24 runs from 4 overs. Jason Gillespie top scored for the Aussies with a mere 24 runs as they were all out for 79 runs inside 64 minutes and only 14.3 overs. England won by 100 runs and Kevin Pietersen was named Man of the Match.

ENGLAND V AUSTRALIA – Only Twenty/20 International
13 JUNE 2005, THE ROSE BOWL, SOUTHAMPTON

Result: England won by 100 runs. *Toss:* England. *Umpires:* NJ Long. JW Lloyds.

ENGLAND			Runs	Mins	Balls	4s	6s
ME Trescothick	c Hussey	b Symonds	41	37	55	5	-
+GO Jones	c Kasprowicz	b McGrath	19	14	17	4	-
A Flintoff	c Symonds	b Kasprowicz	6	5	9	-	-
KP Pietersen	c Hayden	b Clarke	34	18	19	3	1
***MP Vaughan**	c Ponting	b Symonds	0	1	2	-	-
PD Collingwood	c Ponting	b McGrath	46	26	28	5	2
AJ Strauss		b Gillespie	18	16	15	1	-
VS Solanki	c Hussey	b McGrath	9	5	5	1	-
J Lewis	not out		0	0	1	-	-
D Gough	did not bat						
SJ Harmison	did not bat						
Extras	(lb 1, nb 2, w 3)		6				
TOTAL	(8 wickets, innings closed,						
	79 minutes, 20 overs)		179				

FoW: 1-28 (Jones, 3.5 ov), 2-49 (Flintoff, 5.5 ov), 3-100 (Pietersen, 10.5 ov), 4-102 (Vaughan, 11.2 ov), 5-109 (Trescothick, 13.1 ov), 6-158 (Strauss, 18.2 ov), 7-175 (Solanki, 19.4 ov), 8-179 (Collingwood, 19.6 ov)

Bowling	O	M	R	W
Lee	3	0	31	0
McGrath	4	0	31	3
Kasprowicz	3	0	28	1
Gillespie	4	0	49	1
Clarke	3	0	25	1
Symonds	3	0	14	2

AUSTRALIA

AUSTRALIA			Runs	Mins	Balls	4s	6s
+AC Gilchrist	c Pietersen	b Gough	15	14	11	3	-
ML Hayden	c Pietersen	b Gough	6	4	12	1	-
A Symonds	c Pietersen	b Lewis	0	2	5	-	-
MJ Clarke	c Jones	b Lewis	0	1	1	-	-
MEK Hussey	c Flintoff	b Gough	1	6	6	-	-
*R Ponting	c Solanki	b Lewis	0	3	6	-	-
DR Martyn	c Trescothick	b Lewis	4	4	6	1	-
B Lee	c Harmison	b Collingwood	15	20	29	1	-
JN Gillespie	c Trescothick	b Collingwood	24	18	18	4	-
MS Kasprowicz	not out		3	5	16	-	-
GD McGrath		b Harmison	5	12	9	-	-
Extras	(b 1, lb 2, nb 2, w 1)		6				
TOTAL	(all out, 64 minutes, 14.3 overs)		79				

FoW: 1-23 (Gilchrist, 2.4 ov), 2-23 (Hayden, 2.5 ov), 3-23 (Clarke, 3.1 ov),

4-24 (Symonds, 3.4 ov), 5-24 (Hussey, 4.4 ov), 6-28 (Ponting, 5.1 ov), 7-31 (Martyn, 5.5 ov),

8-67 (Gillespie, 10.3 ov), 9-72 (Lee, 12.1 ov), 10-79 (McGrath, 14.3 ov)

Bowling	O	M	R	W
Gough	3	0	16	3
Lewis	4	0	24	4
Harmison	2.3	0	13	1
Flintoff	3	0	15	0
Collingwood	2	0	8	2

─◦ A DANGEROUS AMOUNT OF SUGAR ◦─

Charlie Absolom had an unspectacular England career, playing in one Test match, versus Australia in Melbourne in 1879. However, he gained unforunate notoriety following his cricket career after becoming a ship's purser. On 30 July 1899 Absolom was killed in a freak accident when he was accidentally buried by a misplaced load of sugar while he was loading a ship at Port of Spain, Trinidad.

Ⅲ

"Goochie hadn't used it much and I thought there were a few runs left in it."

Ian Botham on why he used Graham Gooch's bat in his match-winning Headingley innings, 1981 (Gooch made 2 and 0)

≺◦ ENGLAND BEAT SRI LANKA ◦≻

After drawing the First Test at Lord's, England won the Second Test against the visiting Sri Lankans by a six-wicket margin at Edgbaston on 28 May 2006. Sri Lanka won the toss and decided to bat scoring 141 all out in their first innings. England replied with a score of 295 all out. In their second innings Sri Lanka hit 231 all out leaving England requiring 78 runs to go 1–0 up in the three-Test Series. England hit 81 runs for 4 wickets to claim victory. Muttiah Muralitharan claimed all four of England's second innings wickets and ended the match with 10 wickets for 115 runs. Liam Plunkett took an impressive six wickets for only 60 runs in the match. Sri Lanka bounced back to win the Third Test at Trent Bridge to draw the series.

≺◦ THE BIRTH OF THE "GOOGLY" ◦≻

A googly is a type of delivery bowled by a leg-spin bowler and is sometimes referred to as a "Bosie" after its inventor Bernard Bosanquet. Whereas a normal leg-break spins from the leg to the off-side away from a right-handed batsman, a googly spins in the opposite direction, from off to leg, into a right-handed batsman.

Sometime during 1897, Bernard Bosanquet, an all-round cricketer at Eton, Oxford, Middlesex and England, was playing a game with a tennis ball commonly known as "twisti-twosti". The game's objective was to bounce the ball on a table so that your opponent sitting opposite could not catch it. After a few attempted bounces Bosanquet was able to pitch the ball which then broke in a certain direction and then with a similar type of delivery he was able to make the next ball go in the opposite direction.

Following on from this Bosanquet practised the same thing with a soft ball at "Stump-cricket" and finally progressed to using a cricket ball. The googly made its inaugural public appearance in July 1900 when he played for Middlesex against Leicestershire at Lord's. Samuel Coe of Leicestershire became the maiden victim of the googly when Bosanquet had him stumped from a delivery that bounced four times before it hit the wicket. A revolution in bowling was born.

⫼

⟿ WILFRED RHODES ⟿

Wilfred Rhodes was born on 29 October 1877 in North Moor, Kirkheaton, near Huddersfield. Rhodes was without doubt one of the finest cricketers of the twentieth century. His record for Yorkshire and England as a batsman and a spin bowler is perhaps enough to place him as the greatest all-rounder the game has ever seen. What is even more remarkable about his achievements is that he made them at a time when the pitches were very poor, the equipment was less than desirable and diet and fitness were not taken as seriously as they are today.

Rhodes's career statistics include many remarkable achievements: most first-class matches (1,110) and County Championship matches (763) played; the highest aggregate of first-class wickets (4,204); record-holder for taking 100 wickets in a season (23 times, including three seasons when he notched up over 200); record-holder for "doubles" of 1,000 runs and 100 wickets in a season (16 between 1903 and 1926); 12 County Championship winners' medals, all with Yorkshire, between 1898 and 1925; first Englishman and second player overall (after George Giffen) to achieve the "double" of 1,000 runs and 100 wickets in Test cricket; first man to achieve 2,000 runs and 100 wickets in Tests.

Rhodes made his England Test debut in the first Test of the 1899 Ashes series at Trent Bridge – the first ever Test at Nottingham. He scored 6 runs and took 7 wickets in a match England won easily. Three years later Rhodes played in one the greatest ever Test series against the touring Australians. In the first Test of 1902 he took 7 for 17, and at The Oval he helped George Hirst win the final Test by one wicket after an outstanding innings by Gilbert Jessop. In 1903/04, Rhodes toured Australia with the MCC and shone, taking 15 wickets for 124 (despite eight dropped catches) at Melbourne and, going in last, adding 130 with Tip Foster for the tenth wicket at Sydney.

Rhodes rapidly moved up the batting order for Yorkshire and scored his maiden double century against Somerset in 1905. By now his batting was solid and he could be relied upon to score runs in the most difficult of circumstances. In 1907/08 he once again toured Australia, but the unusually humid conditions did not suit him.

In his career, Rhodes scored 39,969 runs at 30.81 and took 4,204 wickets at 16.72. His England statistics, in 58 Test matches, were 2,325 runs at 30.19 and 127 wickets at 26.96. Fittingly for a man who played Test cricket in five decades, Wilfred Rhodes died in his 11th decade, on 8 July 1973, aged 95.

Ⅲ

~ THE GREAT TEST MATCHES (14) ~

Just days before the first Test of England's 2005/06 trip to India, England captain Michael Vaughan sustained a knee injury that ended his tour. Led by stand-in captain Andrew Flintoff, England drew the first Test in Nagpur but lost by 9 wickets in Mohali to trail 1–0 in the three-match series. The deciding third Test took place in Mumbai's Wankhede Stadium, beginning on 18 March 2006.

India won the toss and skipper Rahul Dravid elected to field. England ended the first day on 272 for 3 (Paul Collingwood 11 not out and Andrew Flintoff 17 not out), with Andrew Strauss having scored a superb 128. England went on to make 400, Flintoff recording a half-century and debutant Owais Shah 88. By the close India had reached 89 for 3 in reply (Rahul Dravid 37 not out and Yuvraj Singh 32 not out).

On the third day India were all out for 279, wicket-keeper M.S. Dhoni top-scoring with 64 and Jimmy Anderson taking 4 for 40. Leading by 121 runs going into the second innings, England ended the third day's play on 31 for 2 (Owais Shah 15 not out and Shaun Udal 2 not out). The following day England added a further 160 runs before being bowled out for 191, Anil Kumble taking 4 for 49. India were left with a target of 313 to win and they ended the fourth day on 18 for 1 (Wasim Jaffer 4 not out and Anil Kumble 8 not out), with Irfan Pathan the man out, bowled by Anderson for 6.

Just two wickets fell on the morning of the final day, but then suddenly England took 7 wickets in just 16 overs after lunch to clinch their first Test win in India for 21 years. The tourists secured victory by 212 runs as India subsided from 75 for three to 100 all out. Flintoff took 3 for 14, but the hero was veteran off-spinner Udal, whose figures 4 for 14 were the best in his brief Test career. The series ended tied at 1–1. When interviewed after the win, Udal said: "I've got three children at home. I just timed the wickets before they went to school so they could watch."

Did You Know That?

Mumbai is India's cricketing capital and three different grounds have hosted Test matches. England played in the first Test on Indian soil at the Bombay Gymkhana ground in 1933/34. After World War II, the Cricket Club of India's (CCI) Brabourne Stadium hosted 17 Tests. In 1974, a heated dispute between the CCI and the Bombay Cricket Association (BCA), resulted in the BCA building the 45,000-capacity Wankhede Stadium, which hosted its inaugural Test match in January 1975 when the West Indies toured India.

INDIA V ENGLAND – Third Test

18–22 MARCH 2006, MUMBAI, INDIA

Result: England won by 212 runs. *Toss:* India. *Umpires:* DB Hair and SJA Taufel.

ENGLAND

AJ Strauss	c Dhoni	b H Singh	128	c Dhoni	b Patel	4
IR Bell	c H Singh	b Sreesanth	18	c Dhoni	b Sreesanth	8
OA Shah	c Dravid	b H Singh	88	run out		38
KP Pietersen	c Dhoni	b Sreesanth	39	(5) c & b	b Kumble	7
PD Collingwood	c Dhoni	b Sreesanth	31	(6) c & b	b H Singh	32
*A Flintoff	c Tendulkar	b Kumble	50	(7) st Dhoni	b Kumble	50
†GO Jones	c Kumble	b Sreesanth	1	(8) c Pathan	b H Singh	3
SD Udal	c Kumble	b Patel	2	(4) c Dhoni	b Sreesanth	8
MJ Hoggard		b Patel	0	lbw	b Kumble	6
JM Anderson	c Y Singh	b H Singh	15	c Dravid	b Kumble	6
MS Panesar	not out		3	not out		0
Extras	(b 5, lb 7, w 3, nb 3)		18	(lb 9, w 4, nb 10)		23
TOTAL	(all out)		400	(all out)		191

1/52, 2/230, 3/242, 4/326 5/328
6/333, 7/356, 8/356, 9/385

1/9, 2/21, 3/61, 4/73, 5/85, 6/151
7/157, 8/183, 9/188

Bowling: *First Innings:* Pathan 17–4–64–0, Sreesanth 22–5–70–4, Patel 29–4–81–2, Kumble 39–7–84–1, Harbhajan Singh 26.4–4–89–3. *Second Innings:* Pathan 13–2–24–1, Patel 13–2–39–1, Sreesanth 13–3–30–1, Kumble 30.4–13–49–4, Harbhajan Singh 23–9–40–2.

INDIA

W Jaffer	c Jones	b Hoggard	11		b Anderson	10
V Sehwag	c Shah	b Hoggard	6	(7) lbw	b Anderson	0
*R Dravid	c Jones	b Anderson	52	(4) c Jones	b Flintoff	9
SR Tendulkar	c Jones	b Anderson	1	(5) c Bell	b Udal	34
Yuvraj Singh	c Jones	b Flintoff	37	c Collingwood	b Flintoff	12
†MS Dhoni	run out		64	(8) c Panesar	b Udal	5
IK Pathan	c Hoggard	b Udal	26	(2)	b Anderson	6
A Kumble	lbw	b Panesar	30	(3) lbw	b Hoggard	8
Harbhajan Singh	c Jones	b Anderson	2	c Hoggard	b Udal	6
S Sreesanth	not out		29	not out		0
MM Patel		b Anderson	7	c Hoggard	b Udal	1
Extras	(b 4, lb 7, nb 3)		14	(b 1, lb 7, nb 1)		9
TOTAL	(all out)		279	(all out)		100

1/9, 2/24, 3/28, 4/94, 5/142
6/186, 7/212, 8/217, 9/272

1/6, 2/21, 3/33, 4/75, 5/76
6/77, 7/92, 8/99, 9/99

Bowling: *First Innings:* Hoggard 22–6–54–2, Flintoff 21–4–68–1, Anderson 19.1–8–40–4, Panesar 26–7–53–1, Udal 16–2–53–1. *Second Innings:* Hoggard 12–6–13–1, Anderson 12–2–39–2, Panesar 4–1–15–0, Flintoff 11–4–14–3, Udal 9.2–3–14–4.

⫼
⟋ REFERENCES ⟍
WEBSITES

http://en.wikipedia.org/wiki/List_of_Test_cricket_records ✦ www.cricinfo.com ✦
www.cricketarchive.com ✦ www.cricket-records.com ✦ www.howstat.com ✦ www.
dreamcricket.com ✦ www.cricmania.com ✦ http://en.wikipedia.org/wiki/Timeline_
of_cricket ✦ http://en.wikipedia.org/wiki/List_of_Test_cricket_grounds ✦ http://
en.wikipedia.org/wiki/Test_cricket_hat-tricks ✦ http://en.wikipedia.org/wiki/List_
of_Test_cricket_triple_centuries ✦ http://en.wikipedia.org/wiki/List_of_One-day_
International_records ✦ http://en.wikipedia.org/wiki/Category:Cricket_terminology
✦ http://en.wikipedia.org/wiki/Category:Cricket_dismissals ✦ http://en.wikipedia.
org/wiki/Bowling_%28cricket%29 ✦ http://en.wikipedia.org/wiki/Underarm_delivery
✦ http://en.wikipedia.org/wiki/Leg_before_wicket ✦ http://en.wikipedia.org/wiki/
Bodyline ✦ http://en.wikipedia.org/wiki/Leg_theory ✦ http://en.wikipedia.org/wiki/
Off_theory ✦ www.members.tripod.com/oncc/serv042.htm ✦ http://cricket.indiatimes.
com/trivia/triviaarchive-jan.htm ✦ www.banglacricket.com/History/scorecards.php
✦ www.guardian.co.uk/Archive/Article/0,4273,3894178,00.html ✦ www.lords.org/
laws-and-spirit/laws-of-cricket/ ✦ www.cricinfo.com/link_to_database/SOCIETIES/
ENG/ACUS/ ✦ http://www2.uol.com.br/speakup/stories_b/185_cricket.shtml ✦ www.
safrica.info/ess_info/sa_glance/sports/sports_trivia.htm ✦ http://en.wikipedia.org/wiki/
English_national_cricket_captains ✦ http://en.wikipedia.org/wiki/Cricket ✦ www.
news.bbc.co.uk/sportacademy/bsp/hi/cricket/rules/the_game/html/pitch_dimensions.
stm ✦ http://en.wikipedia.org/wiki/County_Championship ✦ http://en.wikipedia.
org/wiki/C%26G_Trophy ✦ http://en.wikipedia.org/wiki/Twenty20_Cup ✦ www.
cricketworld.com ✦ www.cricketfundas.com ✦ www.answers.com ✦ http://en.wikipedia.
org/wiki/Tied_Test ✦ www.dreamcricket.com/dreamcricket/news/DCNewsDetail.
asp?nid=763&ntid=3 ✦ www.independent-bangladesh.com/news/aug/09/09082005sp.
htm ✦ http://news.bbc.co.uk/sport1/shared/spl/hi/cricket/02/ashes/legends/html/
botham.stm ✦ www.pubquizhelp.34sp.com/sport/personality.html ✦ www.
outlookindia.com/pti_news.asp?id=71164 ✦ www.dimdima.com ✦ http://en.wikipedia.
org/wiki/English_national_cricket_captains ✦ www.mcg.org.au ✦ www.hindu.com ✦
www.334notout.com ✦ http://cricketsociety.com ✦ www.firstscience.com ✦ www.nobok.
com ✦ www.angelfire.com ✦ www.rediff.com/cricket ✦ http://freespace.virgin.net ✦
www.britainunlimited.com ✦ http://en.wikipedia.org/wiki/Andrew_Flintoff ✦ www.
hinduonnet.com/tss/tss2843/stories/2005/022003105800.htm

BOOKS

- *Bodyline Autopsy*, David Frith, ABC Books (2002).
- *Bodyline: The Novel*, Paul Wheeler, Faber and Faber (1983).
- *The Cricket Captains of England*, Alan Gibson, The Pavilion Library (1988).
- *Great Ashes Battles*, Bernard Whimpress & Nigel Hart, Carlton Books Limited (2006).
- *A Social History of English Cricket*, Sir Derek Birley, Aurum Press Ltd (2003).
- *The Ultimate Encyclopedia of Cricket*, Peter Arnold & Peter Wynne-Thomas, Carlton Books Limited (2006).
- *Wisden Cricketers' Almanack*, edited by Matthew Engel, John Wisden & Co. (2005).

JOURNALS

- "A fair method of resetting the target in interrupted one-day cricket matches", FC Duckworth & AJ Lewis, *Journal of the Operational Research Society*, Volume 49, No. 3 pp 220–227 (March 1998).

III

⌐ INDEX ⌐